WN OF MACON

GEORGIA:

OF THE LEGISLATURE,
1822.

BY JAMES SMITH,
OLIVER H. PRINCE,
ABNER WIMBERLY, } COMMISSIONERS.
PLEASANT PHILLIPS,
WILLIAM HAMILTON

WEST COMMO

WEST COMMO

STREET

STREET

STREET

STREET

STREET

STREET

STREET

BRIDGE OR MATTHEWS STREET

RESERVED

SQUARE.

COURT HOUSE SQUARE

ACADEMY SQUARE

FIFTH   FOURTH   THIRD   SECOND   FIRST

STREET

BRIDGE

RIVER

"Until recently the letters and journals around which this story is told were kept folded in an old candy box hidden in the antebellum desk of Washington Poe." So writes Virginia King Nirenstein in the author's note to this charming chronicle of a nineteenth-century Georgia family.

Although the family letters and documents are connected with a narrative to locate them in the time and place of history, the unfolding story is told in a large part through the words written by and to:

Oliver Hillhouse Prince—A Connecticut-born renaissance man who participated in the development of Georgia in many roles. One of the five commissioners sent by the state legislature to lay out the Middle Georgia town of Macon in 1823, he also wrote the story in Augustus Baldwin Longstreet's classic *Georgia Scenes* titled "The Militia Company Drill," which Mrs. Nirenstein includes here.

Mary Norman Prince—Wife of Oliver Prince. Together they perished in a dramatic shipwreck off North Carolina's treacherous Outer Banks.

Washington Poe—Cousin of Edgar Allan Poe, brother-in-law and law partner of Prince, and a delegate to Georgia's Secession Convention. Twice elected mayor of Macon, he was hailed upon his death as one of the town's most influential citizens.

Virginia Prince Green—Elder daughter of the Princes and legal ward of Washington Poe. Studious and literary minded, she and her husband, Dr. James Mercer Green, filled their elegant Macon home with books.

James Mercer Green—Civic leader, founder of the Georgia Academy for the Blind, and Surgeon General of the Middle Georgia hospitals during the Civil War.

Frances Prince King—Virginia's sister. Pretty and vivacious, she married into the founding family of the aristocratic North Georgia town of Roswell and lived there in Barrington Hall, one of the state's famed antebellum mansions.

James Roswell King—Fanny's husband. His fortune and livelihood were destroyed when

With Kindly Voices

Sherman's invading army burned the mills the King family built and operated.

Through the engaging voices of these central characters, *With Kindly Voices* becomes a part of the poignant drama of once-prominent people whose individual destinies paralleled the ante-bellum rise and wartime devastation of Georgia. Upon that stage of history, Mrs. Nirenstein recreates a memorable family.

With Kindly Voices

A Nineteenth-Century Georgia Family

Virginia King Nirenstein

Foreword by Richard Barksdale Harwell

Tullous Books
Macon, Georgia
1984

Published by Tullous Books, P.O. Box 6322, Macon,
Georgia 31208
Printed in the United States of America
LIBRARY OF CONGRESS CATALOGING IN PUBLICATION DATA

Nirenstein, Virginia King, 1930–
  With kindly voices.

  Bibliography: p.
  Includes index.
  1. Prince family. 2. Prince, Oliver Hillhouse, 1782–
1837. 3. Georgia—Biography. I. Title.
CT274.P74N57 1984   975.8′03′0922 [B]   84-8620
ISBN 0-916913-00-7

Designer: Joyce Kachergis
Typeface: Baskerville
Typesetter: G & S Typesetters, Inc.
Printer and Binder: Thomson-Shore, Inc.

Contents

Dear, human books,
With kindly voices, winning looks!
Enchaunt me with your spells of art,
And draw me homeward to your heart.

Oxford Nights, by Lionel Johnson

Illustrations

Author's Note

Until recently the letters and journals around which this story is told were kept folded in an old candy box hidden in the antebellum desk of Washington Poe. There they reposed in Macon for more than a century, unpublished, perhaps not even read by anyone other than their initial recipients. "Specimens" (to borrow Fanny Prince's descriptive term) of a family's handwriting, they have been handed down through four generations.

After I inherited these nineteenth-century manuscripts from my aunt Willie Norman Poe, it became apparent as I began reading and interpreting them that within their content lies the story of one family's significant role in the history of Macon and Georgia. It is my hope that the reader will share with me the charm and, at times, the poignancy of that story. To retain the flavor of these people, I have transcribed their letters and journals as written and left standing occasional doubtful spellings, capitalization, and punctuation. The words the writers underlined for emphasis are underlined here also.

Since this is not a scholarly volume, notes have been kept to a minimum. Only interesting items which expand on the family's history, but which otherwise interfere with the narrative, appear in the notes. Where feasible, however, my sources appear within the text, and at the end of the story is a bibliography.

In performing the satisfying task of preserving this legacy for yet another generation, I have benefited from the advice and assistance of several knowledgeable people. To Richard Barksdale Harwell of Washington, Georgia, I express my heartfelt gratitude for his encouragement and inspiration. I am grateful to Katherine Baker Simpson of Barrington Hall, Roswell, Georgia, for sources of the King family history. In Macon I am indebted to Willard L. Rocker and the staff of the Genealogical and Historical Room of the Washington Memorial Library for help in my research. Finally, I am appreciative of Robert T. Summer's skill in transforming this story into a completed book.

Virginia King Nirenstein

Macon, Georgia
February 1984

Foreword

Books, like people, have kinships with one another. *Vanity Fair* and *War and Peace* are related. *The Leopard* is their Italian cousin, and *Gone with the Wind* is descended from them. The novels of Mary Webb and Constance Holme have much in common, a "connection"—as Southerners say—if not a direct relationship, with those of Kate Chopin and Willa Cather. *Sister Carrie* is a poor relation of *Madame Bovary*, and there is much that *The Red Badge of Courage* shares with *All Quiet on the Western Front* and *What Price Glory?*

Closer home, Eliza Frances Andrews' *The Wartime Journal of a Georgia Girl* can be paired with Mary Boykin Chesnut's *A Diary from Dixie*. Kate Cumming's journal of Confederate hospital life and Louisa May Alcott's descriptions of her work among the Union wounded make the authors sisters under the skin. *The Alexander Letters* is a brother to *The Children of Pride*, and Virginia King Nirenstein's unpretentious volume is very much kin to them both.

Not only are the books akin, the families they represent—the Alexanders, Hillhouses, Lawtons; the Joneses, Dunwodys, Habershams; the Princes, Kings, Greens, and Poes—were kin in some instances, "connected" in others. The Alexanders spread out from Washington, Georgia, to Augusta, Savannah, and widely along the Atlantic seaboard. They were allied in several ways to the Joneses, who themselves populated a considerable portion of Georgia—from Midway and Savannah to Augusta, Roswell, Athens, Marietta, and Rome. Oliver Hillhouse Prince was a close cousin to the Alexanders and, as the reader of this book will see, the bridge between the Alexander and King families.

He was truly a man of Middle Georgia (as the east-central portion of the state was known in the 1800's), ranging in residences and places of particular interest from Washington to Macon, Milledgeville, Athens, and the mountains northeast of Athens. The Kings, who, like the Hillhouses, sprang from Connecticut roots, firmly established themselves in coastal Georgia, created the town of Roswell, and produced a family large enough to spread itself throughout the Confederate army as well as throughout the state. Antebellum Georgia was a state of small population, large families, and long visits. Between them the Alexanders, Joneses, Kings, and Princes were kin to most prominent Georgians and acquainted with the rest.

"Gather up the fragments that remain" was the motto of Thomas H. Wynne, a Richmond antiquarian and book collector who did much to preserve the history of Virginia and the South until the Civil War disrupted his fortune and his collecting activities. Gathering up the fragments is exactly what Virginia Nirenstein has done in working with these family records. Her sources should be described as more than fragmentary, but they lack the bulk that marks the papers of the Alexander family and the several large collections of the Joneses' letters. Perhaps it is good that the Prince-Poe-Green-King collection is not larger than it is. The task of reading the close-written pages of these old letters, much less making out every word of them, is indeed a daunting one. One admires Mrs. Nirenstein's book for what it says, but I must admit my first admiration was for her patience in deciphering such difficult specimens of nineteenth-century handwriting.

Mrs. Nirenstein also had the task of selecting the letters which best carry forward the story of the family and putting them into a context that makes them meaningful to readers not already familiar with the characters and background they represent. But in some areas of the family's history there were hardly enough letters to select from.

The reader is left longing, for example, to know more about James Mercer Green and about Washington Poe and his connection with Edgar Allan Poe.

In addition to letters, the Prince-King collection comprises a group of memorandum books, only one of which is covered at length in Mrs. Nirenstein's text. Three of these little books note the expenses of Prince at different times and the fourth is a cryptic record of his law practice in Macon in 1826. The first expense book is a record of Prince's trip from Washington, Georgia, to Connecticut and back May 16 to November 1813. The second is of a trip by Prince and his wife from Macon to Montreal and back May 8 to October 8, 1830. The last is a record of Prince's expenses in 1832 and 1833, the period during which he moved from Macon and edited the *Georgia Journal* at Milledgeville.

Mrs. Nirenstein wisely includes as an appendix Prince's brief but important sketch "The Militia Company Drill," the "borrowed story" in Augustus Baldwin Longstreet's *Georgia Scenes*. Longstreet noted in the first edition of his book (Augusta 1835): "This is from the pen of a friend, who has kindly permitted me to place it among 'Georgia Scenes.' It was taken from life, and published about twenty years ago."

There is no further record of Prince as an author of fiction. Someday, however, some literary detective may discover among the unsigned pieces in the *Georgia Journal* companions to this landmark piece in the literature of local color.

Richard Barksdale Harwell

Washington, Georgia
February 1984

Part I

Oliver Hillhouse Prince, circa 1820.
Artist unknown.
Photograph by Ken Hill.

Oliver Hillhouse Prince

T he letters and journals of Oliver Hillhouse Prince
now in existence are few in number; only twenty-
three of the former and four of the latter remain. Yet
these few, with old ink script still remarkably legible, reveal
much about the life of a gentleman described in *Men of
Mark in Georgia* as "a lawyer, United States Senator, literary
man and industrial promoter, and one of the brilliant figures in Georgia in the first half of the nineteenth century."

Prince was born in Montville, Connecticut, on July 31,
1782. His mother, Mary Hillhouse, born April 10, 1753,
was the eldest daughter of Judge William Hillhouse. His
father, William Prince, born March 6, 1753, served eight
days in 1775 as a sergeant in Captain Elisha Fox's company,
"which went to the relief of Boston in the Lexington alarm."
William Prince and Mary Hillhouse were married in Montville on May 6, 1775.

The Hillhouse family had long been political leaders in
Connecticut. William Hillhouse, Mary's father, served for
fifty years in the General Assembly of Connecticut during
colonial times and after statehood. He was also a judge of
the Court of Common Pleas for forty years and a delegate
to the Continental Congress from 1783 to 1786.[1]

James Hillhouse, William's son and Oliver Prince's uncle,
was also politically active. Born in 1754, he was a lawyer,
state legislator, and treasurer of Yale College, his alma ma-
ter, from 1782 to 1832. Serving in the Second and Third
Congresses of the United States as a Federalist, he spent
fourteen years in the Senate and five in the House of
Representatives.

In 1810 he became commissioner of the Connecticut

School Fund and found it in an entangled condition. During his fifteen years of management, however, he extricated the fund from its difficulties and increased its assets to $1.7 million of "solid property."[2]

He had been nicknamed "Sachem," meaning Indian Chief, and was known by this sobriquet in Congress and elsewhere. His favorite toast among old friends was "Let us bury the hatchet," which, spoken with a twinkling of the eye, showed he had no lingering bitterness in his heart. The phrase embodied the spirit of his life. It used to be said in the Senate chamber that he kept a hatchet in his desk under the papers and red tape. When the debates in Congress grew personal he was known to take it out and lay it nonchalantly by his inkstand.

In 1796, William Prince moved his family south to Wilkes County in Georgia, where he was appointed headmaster of the Washington Academy. David Hillhouse, Mary Prince's brother, had migrated earlier and was prospering. He owned a plantation, a general merchandise store, and a newspaper, *The Monitor*, in Washington.

When David Hillhouse died in 1803, the newspaper continued to be published by his wife, Sarah, who may have been Georgia's first woman newspaper editor. Although an existing miniature portrait depicts her as delicate and fragile, she was neither. Well educated in New England before she moved south, she reared three children, managed her husband's large plantation, and ran the store he had opened. An early account reports that she often "performed the art of writing there to the amazement of customers." Apparently it was quite unusual on what was then the frontier for a woman to be able to write.

In the early nineteenth century the editor of a weekly was also the person who gathered the news, set it in type, pulled the papers from a heavy manual press, and usually delivered each issue to the subscribers. Sarah, however, was *tering manner of my prospect of election—The principal object of my friends is to introduce me into public notice this year, and thereby assure my election the next. Cousin Oliver has no doubt before this informed you of my ambition to become conspicuous by some means or other, either in a civil or military respect. It is indeed a fact, that if I had not been a married man, I should have marched to the Indian nation a few weeks ago, with the men who went from this county. There are now about 3000 men under arms, encamped on the Ocmulgee river, ready to invade the Creek nation. Savannah is in a dangerous situation—It is expected that troops will be required from the upper country to march to its protection. Our country, therefore seems to have an appearance, but little less hostile than the one you inhabit. I have often sincerely regretted that I had not gone on with Cousin Oliver, and joined the standard of my country, in opposition to the proud foe who now faces our shores, and to those sneaking, toryfied rascals on our own land, who not only refuse to serve their country in its defence, but treacherously supply that foe with the means of annoying our shores & our trades—I have felt as if I should have earn't by good conduct (should occasion have offered) the companion that now becomes the dearest pledge of my life. Whenever we receive letters from O. I almost envy him the pleasure he enjoys in the society of our friends, and in the amusements of visiting, travelling, whortle-berrying, fishing, &c. &c. However, I think I may now give over all thoughts of seeing Connecticut for many years to come. I presume Cousins Sarah & Harriet Hillhouse will be enabled to inform me of the surprizing changes that matrimony wroughts in the disposition of the parties, by the time I shall see them again. I congratulate you my dear aunt on the improvement of your health, which Cousin Oliver says is very great since you have become inured to the severity of the winters in Connecticut. I had designed at first thoughts of writing to have written to Cousin Oliver,* *but fearing that he may have left you, I conclude to write to you only—If he has not yet set off for Georgia, remember us to him. My mother has removed entirely to Mr. Gilberts—Sally lives with me. W. G. is in much the same state of health, that he was when I last wrote to O. We all regret that you are not coming to visit us. Sister Mary sends her love to you—her family of children are well. Mr. S. is not. Mr. S. and myself have at length made up our long existing difference. Remember me, and my Charlotte to <u>all</u> our friends in Montville. Every body here of your acquaintance is well.*

Your affectionate Nephew
D. P. Hillhouse

N. B.   Mrs. Long & Mrs. Telfair desire you should remember them. Mrs. Telfair has a daughter named "Mary Eliza"—Martha Burns is now in Waynesboro'. <u>Major</u> Long has entered the army as a <u>Colonel</u>. Richard is practising law; will soon be married. Mr. Burch continues to keep school—he now has a daughter, and his wife is in a fair way for recovery.

P.S. to my N. B.   Old Fanny has a kind of palsy that has injured her head and arms. Julia lives with Sister Mary and has 2 children—Lotty is sold & moved away—She has one. Maria's children (5 in number) are fine ones—Old Handy & Henly's Jim are in <u>high health</u> and <u>strong spirits</u>! Old Delia is at Burkes, & Old Gabriel preaches yet.

Wilkes was the largest county in Georgia, and by 1790 about half the population of the state had settled there and in the surrounding areas. Most of these settlers had migrated to Georgia by way of the Great Philadelphia Wagon Road, the most traveled route in Colonial America. It ran from Philadelphia to Gettysburg, Pennsylvania, then turned south across the Potomac River at Williamsport, Maryland, and continued down the Valley of Virginia. It followed the

Shenandoah Valley to Roanoke, where it divided. One section of the road went west into Tennessee, but the main road led to Georgia.

Many of the settlers who came to the upper part of Georgia were Virginians. George and Sarah Norman were part of this migration. Bringing with them perhaps their most prized possession, a mahogany drop-leaf table, they settled in Lincoln County in 1795. It was there where the Norman's eldest child was born on December 16, 1798, and christened Mary Ross for her paternal grandmother. The Normans had four other children: Nancy, William, Sarah Ann, and Selina Shirley, the youngest.

At the time of his marriage to Mary Norman, Oliver Prince was considered to be a most eligible bachelor. Handsome, urbane, and a successful lawyer, he was, in addition, an elegantly dressed man of fashion. In the previously mentioned journal, he recorded that on the visit to his mother's family in Montville and New Haven he purchased "morocco pumps, silk stockings, black breeches and silver hooks and links for a great-coat." Among his friends in Washington, he was known as one of the beaux of the town.

On August 15, 1817, Mary Ross Norman, a nineteen-year-old beauty, and Oliver Hillhouse Prince were married by the Reverend Moses Waddel in Lincoln County. The Hillhouse family connections in New England were extensive, and it is likely that letters were exchanged concerning the marriage in the slow and uncertain mails. Unfortunately, any letters Prince wrote to his relatives telling of his marriage did not survive, but two extant letters he received during this time related the sad news of the loss of family members.

The Raymond brothers, David and Daniel, were Prince's first cousins, sons of Rachel Hillhouse Raymond, a sister of Oliver's mother. David's letter informed Oliver of the death of his wife, while Daniel's told of the death of his sister Mary and concern for his brother.

Mary Norman Prince, circa 1820.
Artist unknown.
Photograph by J. Carol Gore.

Paoli Orange County Indiana

Dear Friend,   Oct. 9th 1818

I reached this place my former home, on the 6th inst. after an absence of about six months. In the early part of April last, I descended the Ohio and Mississippi with Mrs. Raymond, who about a month before had been attacked with the symptoms of a consumption. From New Orleans we took passage in a vessel to Baltimore and from thence travelled by the Steam Boat route to Lanningburgh her former home and then the residence of her mother. Having visited our friends in Connecticut we undertook early in the month of August, our return by land to Indiana. We travelled in a waggon Mrs. Raymond had but faint hopes of recovering her health but her desire to see her child, a year old, induced her to undertake the journey. She lived to accomplish but five hundred and fifty miles out of nine hundred. She died in the State of Ohio near to, and was buried at a little village called Canton the County seat of Stark County.

She was an amiable and excellent woman. She possessed native talents and they were cultivated by education. Her society was all that rendered my residence in Indiana pleasant—there was here no society which I enjoyed but hers, nor is there any in this country that can supply its loss.—

I am obliged to you for the letter you wrote me after my marriage, particularly on account of the pleasure it gave my wife, and if I did not answer it as I think I did not I am much to blame.—

It is at present my opinion that I shall not remain in this state. I wish to mingle in new scenes. I think there are places in which I would find better society. I have thought of several places and among others of the southern part of Tennessee, the State of Mississippi, and the Alabama Territory. I have had thoughts of taking a journey into that quarter this winter. Mary informed me that you had thoughts of removing to the Alabama. Should you put your intention in execution I should be glad to know in what part you may fix your residence in order should I take the journey I have slightly contemplated, that I might pay you a visit. I should also like to know whether there are any and what inducements for me to go into that country.

Present my compliments to Mrs. Prince. Also remember me to Cousin David and his wife & to Mr. & Mrs. Shepherd.

Yours with much esteem

David Raymond

O. H. Prince Esqr.

I wish you to write the first leisure hour and send your letter by the way of Baltimore. Letters between me and Mary when she was in Georgia were frequently delayed or miscarried.—

Dear Sir

The foregoing came to me unsealed. I therefore write a postscript. You see D. is still under the influence of his restless disposition. I think it would be better if he was more stable—I hope you will rather discourage his leaving Indiana unless you have strong inducements to the contrary. Give my love to Mrs. P & all friends.—

Yours etc.

D. Raymond

The sadness and despair of David Raymond's letter induced much sympathy for him, and the following letter from Daniel indicates that David had been in Washington for a long visit.

Dear Sir,   *Baltimore, July 27, 1819*

My Brother wrote me the 28th June that he should leave Washington the next day on his return. If he did so the contents of a letter I wrote to him from Montville on the 5th July may not yet be known to our friends in Washington. That letter contained the afflicting news of the death of my sister, Mary. She died on the 1st day of July. Her disease had taken a dangerous turn a few days before and I had been away, but before I arrived home she was dead and buried. Although she had been sometime sick, yet she had not been considered dangerous, and was after her disease became dangerous, it was not expected to prove fatal so soon. She had first the fever and ague . . . her physician thought she might recover. The day before she died she sat up half the day, [and] combed her own head. At the time however she was reduced to mere skin and bones. She perceived great resolution and put the best foot forward during her whole illness. No change for the worst was perceived till 1 oclock in the morning when she awoke from sleep, apparently in a fright or alarmed, called for the servant woman and seemed to be deranged. She sunk away afterwards as if from exhaustion of nature and died in two hours. Thus died a most beloved sister, a most affectionate daughter, and we trust a saint fitted for Heaven. My sister, Debby, arrived home on the 11th July, she was well, though a good deal fatigued with her journey. I wish you to write to me immediately, and give me what information you can respecting my Brother. We supposed from his letter that he had left Washington, but Aunt Hillhouse whom I saw in New Haven said she had had letters as late as the 12th July which did not mention his having left. We feel very uneasy about him. From his letters we had been led to suppose he was in a consumption. From his last letter, however, he appears to be better. But from the manner in which his friends in Georgia have spoken of him to Aunt Hillhouse and others, I suspect he has not been as sick as we supposed, but that he is either [illegible] or is wandering about the country without any reasonable excuse. I wish you to write to me respecting him and tell me the whole truth.

I am instructed by Father to tell you that your money coming from Grandfather's estate will be ready for you this fall, that it would have been ready for you before, if it *could have been got from the Executors, but this has been delayed by a blow-out with them in which they have been defeated. Father also bid me tell you that he had not been able to sell your farm for what he thought it was worth, that he had advertised a long time but no buyers at a fair fee appeared. Mr. Gurley, he says, has offered $1000. for it. Father thinks it is worth $1600 or $1700. If you so direct he will sell it to Mr. Gurley, or he will set it up at auction. You had better instruct him on the subject.*

> *Love to all friends,*
> *Yours etc*
> *D. Raymond*

The year 1820 was a very productive one for Prince. Although there were long days of riding to court through rain and mud, there were other more enjoyable days when he frequently visited his friends in the Georgia legislature, now assembled in Milledgeville, the new capital.

He was well known there and considered a brilliant, capable lawyer. So when the legislators agreed that it was time to prepare another digest of the laws of Georgia, Prince was the man chosen for the assignment.

An order signed by Governor John Clark proclaimed, "Whereas by an Act passed the 21st day of December, 1819 entitled 'An Act prescribing the form of a Digest or Manual of Georgia' it is enacted and declared that during the year eighteen hundred and twenty a Digest of the Laws of this State shall be formed and arranged. . . . And by the same act it is further enacted and declared that the Legislature shall by joint ballot appoint some fit and proper person to arrange a Digest. . . . And Whereas Oliver H. Prince, Esquire, was by joint ballot of both branches of the Legislature in conformity with the before in part recited act, elected on the sixteenth December 1819, to form and arrange a Digest in pursuance of the act aforesaid."

Apparently Prince was elected to prepare the digest five

days before the act calling for a digest passed the legislature. It was an exhaustive task. In the preface of the first edition, Prince reported to Governor Clark: "It would have been as gratifying to myself, as it no doubt would have been to the public if I could have made this report within the time prescribed by the Legislature; but it was impracticable. In a work of such variety and magnitude as that of analyzing and comparing a mass of nearly three thousand acts and resolutions, and culling from them the passages still in force, it is impossible to foresee, with any approach to certainty, what labor may be necessary, or how much time it will consume. I beg your Excellency to be assured, that no sacrifice has been withheld, and no labor and diligence spared, to finish it as early as possible, and to render it useful to the public."

The digest was submitted to the inspection and examination of Judges Cuthbert, Clayton, and McDonald. In their report to the governor, Prince's work was "found to embrace essentially every object contemplated by the law, and is finished in a style of great accuracy and perspicuity." So comprehensive was the first edition, along with the second (1837), of Prince's *Digest of the Laws of the State of Georgia* that it was used by the law profession until 1851, when it was superseded by Thomas R. R. Cobb's. To distinguish one from the other, lawyers called the 1822 first edition *Little Prince*.

Years later, Richard Clark, a prominent Georgia jurist, recalled that one of the vivid recollections of his boyhood was being present in a courtroom and hearing a case argued. The lawyers on both sides frequently read and quoted from Prince's digest. He said that he did not know who Prince was, but in his childish mind thought that he must be the greatest man in the whole state.

The long and laborious task of the digest completed, Prince could now find time to enjoy the company of his two young children, Mary Raymond, born August 21, 1819, and George William, born May 18, 1821. But the happiness the babies brought the parents ended suddenly in tragedy. Both children became ill and died almost a month apart: Mary Raymond on September 15, George William on October 24. The year 1822, which had begun so promisingly, had ended in grief.

It could have been the pain caused by the loss of the children that persuaded Oliver and Mary to leave their home in Washington and migrate farther south in Georgia. Or perhaps it was Prince's memory of the land called the Ocmulgee Fields that he had seen when he went to "fight the proud foe." Whatever the reason, late 1822 found him in the territory of Middle Georgia.

A civil engineer as well as a lawyer, he had been appointed by the legislature in December of that year to head a committee of five commissioners to lay off the metes and bounds of the county of Bibb and the town of Macon. This town was to be situated on the west reserve of the Ocmulgee River near Fort Hawkins, which had been established in 1806 on land ceded by the Creek Indians to the United States. The treaty was signed in the presence of Thomas Jefferson, who, upon the recommendation of Benjamin Hawkins, had insisted upon the privilege of building a fort and trading post on the old Ocmulgee Fields. Although many skirmishes with the Indians occurred over the years, the fort and trading post flourished and settlers began moving into the area.

The Ocmulgee River, or "bubbling waters" as the Indians called it, was even then used for navigation and commerce. Three pole boats were built and served to transport cotton from Jones and Baldwin counties down the river to Darien near Savannah. Charles Bullock and Nicholas Wells established a hotel and store in a double log cabin, while a ferryboat plied its way between the banks of the river. Fort Hawkins, during the Indian Wars of Georgia, was the principal depository for army supplies and troop assignment.

During his military service in middle Georgia, Oliver Prince had earned the rank of major.

The authorization of the Inferior and Superior courts for the new county of Bibb was passed by the Georgia legislature in December 1822. Oliver Prince, already settled near a village afterward known as Holton (and still later as Arkwright), was the only lawyer in the vicinity. On February 15, 1823, the first Inferior Court of the district was held at the house of John Keener, a double log cabin located on land that was later called Beall's Hill. Prince filed the first suit in the court, an action of debt, naming Joseph Kopman vs. Alex Meriwether.

The commissioners appointed by the Georgia legislature to lay off the newly created town of Macon were James Smith, Abner Wimberly, Pleasant Phillips, William Hamilton, and Oliver H. Prince. The survey was made early in 1823 by James Webb, but it was the commissioners who drew the actual plat of the town. The design was in the form of a rectangle with wide streets, supposedly patterned after the symmetrical plan of ancient Babylon. The streets running north and south were named numerically, one to eleven. Those running east and west were called Wharf, Walnut, Mulberry, Cherry, Poplar, Plumb, and Pine. An old Macon newspaper column recorded that *"it was to Oliver Hillhouse Prince's wisdom and foresight that Macon owes her wide streets."*

Lots were to be sold by auction under the authority of the five commissioners, the event advertised in Milledgeville, Augusta, Savannah, and other Georgia newspapers. On the seventh and eighth of March 1823, the auction was held with Thomas Flewellen as auctioneer. The bidding was brisk, and those lots nearest the Ocmulgee River brought the highest prices. Oliver Prince, who planned to open a law office in the new town, later bought a lot on the corner of Fifth and Plumb streets.

Prince, along with David S. Booth, Samuel Wood, and

Charles J. McDonald, was appointed commissioner to govern Macon, which had been incorporated by an act of the legislature. They remained in office for two years.

When the Princes moved from their home in Washington, they brought with them the widowed Mrs. Sarah Norman and her family of four. Since Mary was expecting another child, it was fortunate that her family was with her. When the child—a son—was born on March 16, 1823, they named him Oliver Hillhouse Prince Jr.

A few days earlier, on March 9, Prince had, in company with Judge Eli S. Shorter of Eatonton, started on a trip to Perry, Georgia, to attend Houston County Superior Court. Along with Judge Christopher B. Strong, Charles J. McDonald, Prince's law partner Edward Tracy, and James Smith, they set off in high spirits from their rendezvous in Macon, Thomas Tatum's Inn. Each man, mounted on a good saddle horse, carried in his saddlebag books, papers, a blanket, and lunch. The journey to the small settlement thirty miles south of Macon took almost the whole day. Since there was no road to Perry, the riders were lucky if now and then they found an Indian trail going in their direction. For the most part they were riding in dense forest, but they were all pioneers with as deep a knowledge of woodcraft as of Blackstone.

About one o'clock they forded Ichuccona Creek (present day name Echeconnee), took the saddles from their horses, tied them loosely for a rest, and sat down to eat lunch. Afterward they resumed their journey, now and then in an open glade through which they could canter, but mostly winding their way through the woods at a slow pace. About five o'clock Colonel Smith thought he heard a dog bark and a little later they all heard the sound of an axe. Coming upon a clearing they saw before them a double log house. Inquiring for the house of Jacob Little, the place the legislature had appointed for holding the Houston Superior Court, they were directed there by the settler. Little's house, also a double log cabin (two rooms with a passage between), was built of fresh hewn logs, the cracks between the logs filled with clay, and had a chimney built of large stones. The windows, fitted with stout shutters, looked out on a porch with a shelf at one end which held a bucket of spring water, a tin basin, a gourd of soft soap, and a drinking gourd. In the backyard stood another single log house, used as a kitchen, and nearby a barn and stable. The group, washing away the travel grime at the basin, were then ushered into the largest room where a blazing log fire crackled up the large chimney. Servants pulled a long table into the middle of the room where the distinguished visitors were served a meal of roast leg of venison, hoecakes, sweet potatoes, and sassafras tea. After supper pipes were lit and everyone settled back to enjoy the lively conversation of politics, gossip, and the tall tales of Oliver Prince, "a man of infinite jest and in wit excelled only by Judge John M. Dooley."

The opening of the court on Monday was a red-letter day in the county. Business was suspended as the settlers came in from the surrounding area, often bringing their wives and children. Here was a good opportunity to trade horses, collect debts, and enjoy the trials. If there was a politician running for office, it was a good chance for him to meet a large number of people and campaign a bit. The court itself furnished much news of the outside world. These early sessions of the Superior Court were generally conducted with great formality. A few minutes before the court convened, the sheriff escorted the judge to the place where the court was to be held (usually a log cabin residence of one of the prominent citizens of the town), holding in his hand a long staff and crying as he went, "Make way for the Court, make way for the Court." With his hat on his head, the sheriff walked in front of the judge, pounding the floor with his staff and calling for order. When the judge was seated on the bench, the sheriff opened court with the ancient announcement "Oyez, Oyez. The honorable Superior Court of Houston County is now open." Court now begun, the judge directed the sheriff to call the jurors into the room. With this order, the sheriff went to the window and, in a voice that could be heard for half a mile, shouted, "Jurors come into court and take your seats." A large number of jurors waited outside to be called. Many cases were heard in the three days the court convened. Justice was harsh and swift, and the briefs heard before the courts ranged from property litigation to cold-blooded murder.

As soon as the business in Houston was finished Judge Shorter and his band of lawyers set out for Knoxville, Crawford County, where the next circuit court was held.

About fifty days in the spring and fifty days in the fall, Oliver Prince was kept busy going from court to court.

In the early spring of 1825, Macon prepared for a visit from the French hero of the American Revolution, the Marquis de Lafayette. The sixty-eight-year-old general was visiting America and his triumphant tour lasted many months. He was invited to stop at Milledgeville, where plans were made to entertain him lavishly. When Lafayette left America after the Revolution to return to his home in France, Georgia was a wilderness inhabited by few white people and Milledgeville was not even on the map. But in 1825 it was the capital of the state.

Governor George Troup ordered a military escort for the general upon his arrival at Savannah. Coming into Milledgeville on Sunday, March 27, 1825, General Lafayette, in a barouche drawn by four beautiful bay horses, was escorted by the Hancock and Baldwin County Cavalry. In the town he was greeted by a salute fired from a cannon, the ringing of church bells, and enthusiastic cheering. The Government House was chosen for the lodging, and there a number of little girls of the town scattered flower petals as the Revolutionary hero entered. Later in the afternoon the Methodist church was filled to capacity when Governor Troup and General Lafayette arrived for a special service.

Monday morning at a reception the general was introduced to a few survivors of the Revolution, the members of the Masonic Lodge, and Milledgeville citizens and officials. An elegant banquet that night was followed by a ball lasting until three o'clock in the morning. The general retired to his lodgings at ten o'clock, however, since he was scheduled to leave early the next day for his visit to Macon.

Macon, the growing little village of 750 inhabitants, could not hope to duplicate Milledgeville's elaborate festivities. Its best efforts were simpler, but equally as enthusiastic. At twelve noon, March 29, a signal gun was fired, announcing the approach of Lafayette's carriage. He was accompanied only by his son George Washington Lafayette, his secretary Monsieur Le Vasseur, and two governor's aides, Colonels T. G. Holt and H. G. Lamar. The general left his carriage and crossed by ferry to Macon's Bridge Street (now Fifth Street), where he was welcomed by a committee. Escorted by perhaps the entire population of the town, he walked to his quarters at the Macon Hotel at the foot of Mulberry Street. The visit by Lafayette to the town lasted for only two and a half hours.

Dinner was served by the hotel's host, George Stoval. Ambrose Baber, the Macon Masonic Lodge's Master, toasted the general, who was introduced to everyone present. Lafayette responded to this hospitality with a toast of his own: "The town of Macon; may its prosperity continue to be one of the strongest arguments in favor of republican institutions."

Shortly after dinner, the general left to resume his tour. He was accompanied by the committee, the commissioners, and many other townspeople—all on horseback—for several miles on the road. Lafayette's destination was the Creek agency on the Flint River where he was scheduled to spend the night.

In 1824, barely a year after Macon was incorporated into a town, its commissioners established a school on the square reserved for this purpose. Although Oliver Prince was a trustee for the academy and intensely interested in its welfare, he was not present at the trustees' first meeting held in November 1825. He had good cause for his absence, however; on November 23, 1825, a daughter was born to the Princes.

Sarah Virginia Prince was to become her father's favorite child. His pride in her can be seen in the letter in which he refers to her as a "scholar, almost a blue-stocking, who is seldom seen without a book in her hand." Of all his children, Virginia was the most studious. She learned French at an early age, and because of her scholarship five leather volumes of world geography were especially bound for her by Prince. His last recorded words were a message to Virginia.

By January of 1826, Macon's population had grown to almost eight hundred people. The town had thirty-two stores and was building a new market house in the center of Fifth Street between Cherry and Mulberry. Stalls in the market were offered for rent, and many beautiful elms and oaks were planted along the streets by Simri Rose.

Oliver Prince's law practice was very successful, although he was in constant need of new law partners. Edward Tracy, also a native of Connecticut and his first partner, was elected Macon's first Intendent (mayor) in 1826. Washington Poe, Prince's next partner and future brother-in-law, was chosen Macon's Intendent in January 1827.

The fall of 1828 found Prince again in Milledgeville. Though he had represented Bibb County repeatedly both in the House and Senate of the Georgia legislature, he was preparing to investigate the political scene and campaign for a judgeship. His cousin, David Hillhouse, also active in

Georgia politics, wrote in answer to an inquiry he had received from Oliver.

Dear Sir,   *Washington (Ga), 29th Oct. 1828*
   My almost continual absence during the summer past, prevented the reception of your letter of the 17th July, until late in August—and then there was no opportunity afforded of making the inquiry you desired. An effort was made in this county to run in a partial Troup ticket which wholly failed, as you have learnt. I have had to use much caution in obtaining information upon the subject you desired—and have not been able to succeed (as I think) until a few days ago. I have obtained nothing like a pledge—but am certain that Brown will support you for the Bench, if McDonald is not a candidate—and will use his influence to induce the other members from this county to do so. & I believe that Wooten and Willis are inclined to aid you.
   I have understood that the Lincoln members (one of whom is Barkesdale, that married Thos. Anderson's daughter,) will also support you and I am induced to expect that you will succeed, if you are not out-generaled. A <u>little</u> attention to the Clark folks—not of too marked a character—will secure you their aid, I suspect. But I hope you will not court it so as to give them a claim upon <u>you</u>.
   I should like dearly to be at Milledgeville to <u>see</u> the contest—without <u>hearing</u> it. Altho' I have no wish to divest myself of my political partialities I have to become sobered enough to wish to avoid their prejudices toward men. The more I see of political men, the less I think of their integrity and the less I care to cultivate their acquaintance. For the same reason that I like to see ram-goats contending for a stump, I wish to witness the contested elections for the judgeships.
   Lucy has spoken <u>again</u> of a desire to make Cousin Mary a visit. I wish her to go about the middle of November for we should like to be the first who paid our respects to Judge

Prince and his lady. After an interval of 4½ years, we have
engaged in housekeeping at Waterloo, for this winter only.
But everything is out of place, and my wife has great per-
plexity in renewing her favorite employment.

Lucy desires an affectionate remembrance to Cousin
Mary & yourself & Mrs. Norman & others of your family in
which she is heartily joined by

Your friend
David P. Hillhouse

I feel very anxious for Judge Clayton's re-election (rather
restoration). I am afraid he will be sorely pestered by Dr.
Tinsley who is about to make a desperate effort to injure
him with his (C's) own party. I wish you, or some friend of
the two would endeavor to allay the violence, or at least
confine T's operations to the Clark party.

Whether Prince was ever elected a judge is unknown, but
in that same year he was elected or appointed to fill the un-
expired congressional term of Thomas W. Cobb.

The winter of 1828 in Macon was a most unusual one.
The weather was unseasonably warm, inducing vegetables
to grow and flowers to bloom in the gardens. During this
time the Princes's fifth and last child, Elizabeth Frances,
was born on November 7, 1828, at their home on Fourth
Street (now Broadway). Promptly nicknamed Fanny, she
was from the beginning a cheerful and beautiful child. She
and her sister Virginia, three years apart in age, were always very close.

Shortly afterward Prince went to Washington to serve his
term in Congress. This 20th Congress, held in the waning
days of the presidency of John Quincy Adams, extended
from December 1, 1828, until March 3, 1829.

Adams, defeated by General Andrew Jackson in the
Electoral College, addressed the last session of Congress in

a message reviewing the condition of the country, domestic and foreign relations, and for the first time the subject of the controversial tariff. This tariff had produced much opposition, especially in the South, since it was believed to be a tax on imports of manufactured articles and woolen goods. For the agricultural South, it made the purchase of these items very expensive. As a protest against the tariff, the Georgia delegates appeared in Congress dressed in clothes made from homespun cloth.

On March 4, 1829, Andrew Jackson became the seventh President of the United States. At twelve o'clock the Senate was convened by his predecessor, John Quincy Adams. Jackson entered the Senate chamber escorted by the District Marshal and the Committee of Arrangements. He had come from Gadsby's Hotel accompanied by a few of the surviving officers and soldiers of the Revolutionary War. The new President addressed his remarks to these men and to the other members of the audience, composed of Supreme Court justices, foreign ministers and their colorful entourage, members of the House and Senate, and a large number of ladies, thanking "the companions of the immortal Washington" for their "affectionate message" delivered earlier to him at his hotel.

After the adjournment of the Senate, Andrew Jackson, from the steps of the Capitol, delivered his inaugural address before an immense crowd of spectators. Chief Justice John Marshall administered the oath of office, and the crowd, breaking through the barriers, rushed forward to shake the hand of the President. Cheering crowds followed him as he rode on horseback to the President's House. "Country people, farmers, gentlemen mounted and dismounted, boys, women and children black and white, carriages, wagons and carts all pursuing him" was how one observer saw it. Such a crush developed at the reception held at the President's House that many visitors had to exit through the windows.

The inauguration was symbolic of the times. Gone was the aristocracy of past presidents; General Jackson was the people's choice, a man of democratic principles. Oliver Prince perhaps surveyed the scene thoughtfully as he prepared to return to Georgia.

In the spring of 1830, the notorious author Anne Royall visited Macon. (She had been tried in 1820 and convicted as a "common scold.") During her visit, she was entertained by the politicians and literary men of the town. Her hotel, Washington Hall, completed in 1827 at the corner of Mulberry and Second streets, had as its first proprietors a Mr. Moreland and Mr. Townsend. Mrs. Royall was much pleased with "Mr. Tawnsen." Heaping praise upon him, she withheld her usual caustic abuse.

A prolific writer who had published ten volumes of her travels (*Sketches of History, Life and Manners in the United States*), she had many friends in high places and even more powerful enemies who abhorred the reckless boldness of her pen. In 1831 Mrs. Royall published a periodical, *The Huntress*, in which she wrote many personal pen sketches of the public figures of her day, including some prominent Georgians. Oliver Hillhouse Prince was the subject of one of the sketches. Of her visit to Macon, Mrs. Royall observed that "it was the most flourishing, wealthy, and polite town of its age in the United States."

The journey that Mary and Oliver Prince undertook on May 8, 1830, carried them a long way from Macon. Their route north can be charted from a meticulous record Prince kept in a small memorandum book, where he noted that he left home with $1,649.88½. After paying the $.50 toll at the new bridge in Macon, his first large expenditure was "$24.00 stage fare to Savannah." On May 12 in Savannah he purchased tickets for their passage by ship to New York. The fare was $60.00. Apparently there was a waiting period for the ship to depart, for he wrote that he gave Mrs. Davenport $17.00 for board. After buying gingersnaps, books, lemons (for seasickness), and soda powders, they sailed on May 19. They arrived in New York on May 29, and after a night at a hotel they did some sightseeing, as he noted "Academy of Fine Arts $1.12½, Peal's Museum $.50, Theatre $2.00." Their next stop was Albany, New York (passage $4.00), for a short visit to Oliver's uncle William Hillhouse and cousin David Buel, who lived in nearby Troy. Traveling back and forth between the two towns (fare $.25), Mary and Oliver took the opportunity to shop.† After visiting the Albany and Troy relatives for almost three weeks, the Princes took passage to Schenectady, Utica, Syracuse, and Rochester for a total fare of $20.12. After spending the night at Rochester, they were on their way to Niagara Falls. Their passage to Lockport, New York, was for the amount of $5.12½, and following an overnight stay there on June 23 they hired a hack for Lewiston and Niagara Falls. Lewiston was apparently too small a village to spend much time in, the lure of the falls notwithstanding, for a notation read, "fare from Falls to Buffalo $2.00," and at Buffalo they made their headquarters for more visits to Niagara Falls, staying three days in all.

On the last day of June, they crossed over into Canada: "Passage to Prescott $20.00—Stage from Prescott to Montreal—$14.00."

In Montreal much sightseeing was done, for after visiting a convent where they purchased a "pin-cushion of the nuns $.25," Oliver noted that he spent "$.10 for mending shoes." Paying their hotel bill of $9.60, they left Montreal to take passage on a boat up the St. Lawrence River to Quebec ($8.00). Spending only one day there, they returned to Montreal (passage $10.00) to shop. Coat ($22.00),

---

†"Marino Shawl $14.00, handed Mary $10.00, horsekin boots $2.50, 2 collars .75, ½ doz butter knifes $6.00, 1 black stock $1.50, frock $17.50, letter paper $.18¾, trunk, $12.00 overalls $7.00, suspenders $1.00, articles purchased of the Shakers $4.81½, crimson cloth $7.50, a small wicker wagon $87½, wicker work at Shermans $11.12½, gum elastic over shoes $1.50, cloak bag $3.25."

waistcoat ($3.50), almanac ($.12), tobacco box ($1.46), and a hotel bill of $8.00 were the expenditures of July 8.

Steamboats were in abundance on the rivers of Canada in 1830, and the Princes, evidently enchanted, took passage on one (fare $8.00) and arrived again in the United States at Burlington, Vermont.

From Burlington they made the journey to Boston by stage with two overnight stops and arrived there on the thirteenth of July. They purchased two pairs of boots at $3.25, one pair of kid shoes at $1.00, and two pairs of children's shoes (one pair red), paid the bill at the Tremont Hotel ($13.19), bought Mary a riding habit ($16.86), and took the stage to Providence, Rhode Island, on July 15.

From Providence the stage took them to Norwich, Connecticut, where after purchasing port wine ($.50) for Oliver and cologne water ($.25) for Mary, they spent the night ($10.00). As the fare to Montville, where some of the Hillhouse family still resided, was only $1.00, they went home for a visit, for the expense book did not resume until July 27.

After more shopping and a short stay at Saratoga Springs, the fashionable spa in upstate New York, the Princes boarded a steamboat on September 8 and sailed for New York City. The fare was $4.00 for what was evidently an overnight voyage, as Oliver noted that supper on the steamboat was $.75. On the tenth of September, after purchasing paper for $.18¾ cents, he wrote the following letter to his daughter Virginia, left behind in Macon. She was five years old and the letter, written in a large flowing hand, was short and easy for a child of that age to understand. Mary added a note on the reverse side.

My dear Virginia   *New York, Sept 10th 1830*
   Your mother and I are now a great way from our dear Virginia but we shall soon begin to go towards Macon because we want very much to see her. We hope to hear when we get home that you have been a good girl and been al-

*ways kind to little Frances. You must never take your play-
things from her so as to make her cry. I write this letter to
you because you are father's eldest daughter. I do not write
to Frances because she is so small that she would not know
what it meant.*

Your affectionate Father
O. H. Prince

My dear Virginia
   *I have not time to write much to you but I hope to see
you soon and hear you have been good.*

Mary R. Prince

The serious shopping spree in New York began on September 11, when Oliver recorded that he bought:

Dressing Bureau	$17.00	Sofa	$70.00
Bedstead	17.00	2 Footstools	4.00
Looking Glass	35.00	Backgammon Table	3.75
Fender	7.00	Brass Fender	12.00
Sec. & Bookcase	50.00		

Taking time out for a trip and dinner at Flushing (steamer
over and stagecoach back), they resumed their shopping on
the fifteenth, but not before Oliver had his shoes repaired
again (cost $.12½).

Buying his wife and children many new clothes, he finally resolved that he needed *new* shoes (cost $5.50). After
directing that the newly purchased furniture be shipped to
Savannah, Oliver and Mary took passage to Philadelphia
on September 17. Staying overnight in Philadelphia, Oliver
purchased his one extravagance—books—at Necklings
bookshop for $7.50 and at Smally's for $44.00.

When they left Philadelphia their destination was Baltimore, where they spent the night at the Indian Queen.
On September 20, the journal noted, "Fare to Washington
$4.00." In the capital city they did some sightseeing, and

the next day Oliver listed the expenses of the day as "tobacco $.06¼, crackers $.06, shaving $.06¼, Gadsby's bill $4.00, Hack $1.00, Porter at Presidents house $.25, and fare to Fredericksburg $8.50."

During the two days in Washington, Prince appears to have visited President Andrew Jackson, as the notation of his tip to the porter at the "Presidents house" indicates. Jackson had been at Fort Hawkins during the Indian uprising, and Prince had met the general during the time he was in Washington serving in Congress. Unfortunately, Oliver did not record what the two discussed.

On September 22, Oliver and Mary began the first leg of their journey back home to Macon. In Fredericksburg, Virginia, they paid $33.50 fare to Caswell Court House (Milton) in North Carolina. It would take more than two days to reach their destination since it was 208 miles from Fredericksburg. Perhaps because there were no stages at Milton going in the direction they wished, a hack was hired to take them to Hillsboro, North Carolina, a distance of thirty-five miles. From Hillsboro the stage's route led through Greensboro, Lexington, and Salisbury to Charlotte. On October 2, the Princes were breakfasting in Charlotte. The trip home to Macon would take six more days and as many nights spent in inns along the way.

The old towns in South Carolina that the stage passed through were Pinkneyville, Yorkville, and Union. During this portion of the trip, Oliver recorded in his journal that he purchased a Bible dictionary for $1.00 (perhaps to while away the long hours).

From Abbeville the road led to Washington, Georgia, which the weary travelers reached on October 6. On October 8 the journal noted, "Fare to Macon $6.00," and so they were home at last. They had been away exactly five months to the day. In his journal Oliver estimated (very accurately) the distances between each town, totaled the number of miles, and concluded that they had traveled 4,408 miles on their journey, and spent $1,493.

Instead of his usual large, careless script, he wrote precisely on the final page of his journal: "Note—Our passage fare in stages, steam boats etc from N. York to Albany—Niagara, Kingston, Montreal, Quebec, Burlington, Boston, N. Haven, Albany & back to N. York averages 3½ cents per mile. From N. York by Phil$^{\underline{a}}$, Balt. & Washington to Fredericksburg 4 cents per mile. Through So. Car. & Geo$^{\underline{a}}$ 8½ cents pr mile. From Fredericksburg to Macon upper route 8 cents per. mile."

In 1830, Macon's population was almost two thousand, and there were over one hundred wholesale and retail stores. The little settlement called Newtown around Fort Hawkins had been incorporated into the young town of Macon, where there were two hundred homes, four banks (one of which had Prince as a member of its board), three public schools, and two weekly newspapers.

In the winter Oliver Prince wrote to Thomas Hillhouse in Albany, New York, asking his uncle to help M. J. Slade, a businessman who planned to establish a third newspaper in Macon.

Dear Uncle,   *Macon, Dec. 30 1830*
A Mr Slade of this place is about to go to N. York and probably to Albany to purchase types & materials for a printing office; and I have given him a letter of introduction to you presuming you would like to see a person directly from Macon & feeling myself a pleasure in sending our affectionate greetings by a person who will personally deliver them. After I had written the letter, he requested me to ask for him your assistance if he should want it, in obtaining a credit for a part of his purchase, say 2, 3, or 400 dollars: but not in any way of guarantee—suggesting also

that I should state to you his situation plainly and candidly. For this I take a separate letter—more particularly as I am disposed to write independantly of his affairs.

Mr. Slade & his wife, each of them inherited a good property. He engaged some years ago & has since assisted in conducting a newspaper in this place. He lately failed however & sold out his part of the printing establishment and is now about to set up another, much larger than the former. Who backs him in this new undertaking, I do not know having never inquired. I suspect it is his father-in-law, who is wealthy.

He is an amiable man, of fair standing, of respectable and some of them wealthy connections. He is moreover I think in his principles and intentions an honorable upright man. If he should obtain credit as far as I have mentioned, I confidently believe it will be paid. If I did not think so I would not give him any aid in procuring it. Of course however you will take care not to incur any responsibility.

I have received yours of the 15th Nov^{er} <u>written in the strip</u>, that fact really surprised me. The weather must have been warm indeed for that latitude. With us it has been, with very little exception, not warm but hot—uncomfortably hot, particularly in the middle of the day ever since we returned till about 2 weeks ago when we had the mercury down to 10 Farrenheit it is said—I did not see it. But it has now moderated. I took a slight fever soon after our return, from an incautious exposure to the midday sun in driving to court, and Mary has had a most uncommonly severe attack of the influenza which I presume was from the cold. It confined her to her bed several days and to her room several more. She is now just getting about. Our children have been generally well. Judge Buel has not yet arrived, but he informed me from Raleigh on 16th of this month that his health was good, that he & Mr. B. were getting on comfortably but for the bad roads from the late rains, by which their progress had been retarded. He expected to be in Au-

gusta about this time but as he will previously stop at Washington and several other places, it may be 2 or 3 weeks before we see him. I shall not incur Aunt's heavy rebuke, by <u>*expressing*</u> *a hope that we may someday see you at the South; but she has too much charity to blame me for* <u>*feeling*</u> *it. The desire of revisiting the scenes of other days is common to us all I believe; and we as commonly, I believe, experience a sentiment or feeling something like disappointment in doing so.* [Part of letter torn off.] *. . . that even tho' the scene lives on the people and objects are not as we left them in affectionate remembrance and tho' the wish is to find them the same we know it is hopeless and we find a rigid and uncompromising reality* [illegible] *& more especially in the people* [illegible], *the prevailing feeling is disappointment but it is a disappointment we would not be willing entirely to forego & produces a sadness though not unmixed with pleasure. It is like the music of Carril, pleasant & mournful to the soul.*

Remember us most affectionately to Aunt and Sarah Ann and the boys "each and every one of them" as we say in law,—and our friends in Troy if you think of it. Mary says, and truly enough, that Sarah Ann, who has so little else to do, might write to her. And <u>*I*</u> *say as to the boys that in my long settled opinion, you are right in thinking they ought to go to school from home. I would send Oliver from home even to an inferior school. Mary sends to you her kind and affectionate remembrance in which she is joined by*

Yr Affectionate Nephew
O. H. Prince

[Torn part of letter discusses a potato which Mary has grown in her garden and its large circumference.] *The potatoe she mentions is not now in existence. She insists on my sending you the account—She wishes she could send Aunt the potatoe*

O.H.P.

Apparently Slade succeeded in his efforts, for on February 15, 1831, he issued a semiweekly newspaper, the *Macon Advertiser, Mercantile and Commercial Intelligencer.*

The subject of the building of railroads in Georgia had been on the minds of many citizens of Macon for eight years. There was much talk but no action was taken until 1831. In August of that year a public meeting was held at the courthouse to appoint delegates to Georgia's first railroad convention, which was to be held at Eatonton. The convention's purpose was to decide on the mode of transportation best suited for the state. Oliver Prince and Dr. W. B. Rodgers were chosen as delegates from Bibb County, and Prince was named chairman of the convention.

Being deeply interested in the rail system of transportation, Prince was one of the first stockholders and directors of the earlier established Georgia Railroad Company of Augusta. Macon's own railroad, however, was not built until 1838.

In the early months of 1832, Oliver Prince closed his law office in Macon and moved to Milledgeville to become the owner and editor of the *Georgia Journal.* Prince purchased James Camak's interest in the newspaper, and partner Thomas Ragland, who owned the other half-interest in the paper, continued in his role of junior editor. On December 29, 1831, Camak made the announcement in the paper that "the sale of my interest in the Journal office to Mr. O. H. Prince will take date from the 1st of next month. At his request however I will continue my agency in the management of the paper until he can prepare for his removal to Milledgeville which will be in the course of next month." The 1832 journal Prince kept for his expenses in Milledgeville noted that on January 17 he "gave the boys $1.25 for moving boxes, desk, etc. to the office." Finding it difficult to secure acceptable lodgings in the crowded capital, he did not move his family immediately from Macon, apparently commuting between the two towns until July 1832.

On February 2, 1832, Prince issued his statement of policy in the *Georgia Journal*:

I believe it is the Spanish people who have a proverb that "the host carries the table cloth" a free translation of which may be; that the guest can generally form a judgment from first appearances, what kind of fare he will find in the House.

Now it would be unfortunate if this proverb was to apply to a new editor whose prefatory article made up, as it commonly is, of truisms and egotisms is apt to be the very flattest dish he ever offers. But what cannot be well avoided must be encountered. The patrons of the paper have a right to know the principles and opinions of him who expects to take so large a share in its future editorial management. And this being the first number in which that agency commences; it seems to present the proper and perhaps the only appropriate occasion for a word from himself individually, to its readers, with a perfect understanding which ought if possible to exist between them.

The tendency of every press should undoubtedly be to virtue, truth and justice. It should seek to elevate the morals, to purify the tastes, to inform the judgment, and defend the interests of the people.

The periodical press will most certainly and directly accomplish these objects by truth and candor in fact and argument, by a denial of its columns to vice and immorality in all its forms: by requiring that all, if possible, which it offers, be written in good taste and good temper; by seeing that the current of its information be regular and authentic; and by assuming and steadily defending, with equal temperance and firmness which political doctrines and maxims as best promote the greatest lasting good.

We all agree, or profess to agree, in these general princi-

ples. Our dissentions commence with their specific application. And in this there shall be no mistake between us, if I
can prevent it. The opinions I have long held on the leading questions of policy which now most interest the public
mind are, I believe, well known to those who know me.
They have been freely expressed in social intercourse; and
wherever occasion required have been acted on in such
part as I have taken in public affairs. Indeed a confession
of faith in all proper form would be soon dispatched: for
my doctrine, or the doctrine as I understand it, of strict
construction ascertains and determines most of the rest. It
denies to Congress equally the right to bestow internal improvements on the States and to inflict a tariff of bounties
on the people of the States under any qualification of limit.
In one of these it has sinned against the letter, and in the
other, against the spirit of the constitution. It denies also the
charter to a national Bank which, under any modification
that I have seen proposed, would do violence both to the
letter and spirit of that instrument. It asserts the sovereignty of the States; but it deprecates nullification: because
with the sovereignty it inculcates with equal earnestness the
Union of the States and will never "give it up" until it aban-
dons the hope that free governments can exist upon the
earth. My voice in support of the present incumbent for
the next term of the presidency, is not given solely, or even
principally, for his services in the field, illustrious as they
were. Gratitude is one sentiment, and confidence is another. But I shall support him because of the firmness, the
straight-forward frankness, the activity and vigor of his
past administration; and more especially because his measures have pledged him to axioms of policy which I deem
safe and salutary.

The political position of this State is perhaps at this time
more intensely interesting than that of any other member
of the Union; from the single fact that her local affairs, her
Indian relations for instance, have been pressed into the

*general politics of the country and made prevading party
questions. Now it has ever seemed to me, that for this nation to discuss the question, whether the people of Georgia
shall or shall not occupy the present Indian lands within
her limits, is just as idle as to discuss the expediency of the
tides or of wind or rain—The event must inevitably happen. What course, whether hostile or pacific, would or
could the government adopt, that would not end in that
final result? Considering that event, then, as an invincible
necessity, which it certainly is, the legitimate province of
the general and State governments surely is, to modify and
direct that tide of events which cannot be controlled and
shape their measures on this, as on every other complex
question, for the greatest good and least injury to the parties concerned. Let Georgia firmly and steadily assert and
act up to her acknowledged rights; thus much is due to her
interests. Let her at the same time, carefully respect the
rights of the Indians; thus much she owes to her character.
Let these be done, and both branches of the problem will
be solved. She will obtain what she claims and she will obtain it without reproach.*

*Our representation should be reduced. A Court for the
correction of errors should be established. It is too late
in the day to resume the barbarous punishments of the
old common law. We should keep continually before the
people the incalculable importance of internal improvement. For next to the vindication of principle, that is the
greatest service we can render to the present generation.
And we should promote education as the greatest possible
good to posterity—It is the only aliment of our future
strength.*

*Selections must of course be governed by the purpose
and objects of the publication. A journal conducted on as
general a plan as this is, must necessarily assume as miscel-
laneous a character as possible. Addressing itself to every
taste, and enacting its influence on every interest of so-*

ciety—, it should comprehend within its range, the largest and smallest, the weightiest & the lightest subjects, whether scientific, political, tasteful or merely pleasant, from the profoundest investigations of the frame and action of the government, down to the anecdote of yesterday. A gazette, however is not conceived to be the proper theatre of theological discussion. And if it be there is now no deficiency of papers devoted exclusively to that subject.

An editor's accountability to the public entitles him to a knowledge of the real names of his correspondents; and invests him with the absolute right of refusing to publish whatever in his judgement, ought not for any reason to appear. A decently written article on a matter of public concern may bear hard on some of his esteemed friends; and he may not feel at liberty to reject it on that account for the public interests must not be postponed to the partialties of private friendship. But such friends will always recollect, that the paper is equally open for their reply.

I have spoken of consulting every taste. The remark must of course be understood as confined to every just and proper one. If any of our readers expect the Journal should it be engaged in the warmest contests, will administer to a depraved appetite for licentious ribaldry, and low vituperation, it is but fair to apprise them that they will be disappointed. Such language is below the decent dignity of any well conducted paper; and an editor who habitually indulges in it, ought not to be admitted within the pale of discussion. Reason and truth and sometimes ridicule are the lawful weapons of controversy, and these have the greatest effect when used with decorum. The best polished weapon makes the deepest incision. Persons often scold and call names across a state or continent who perhaps would be very civil if sitting face to face. The laws that should govern the intercourse of gentlemen are always & everywhere the same. The rule should be, to address a distant correspondent as if he were personally present—But will these quiet fire-side reflections in night gown and slippers hold, when the storm shall come, if it does come? Who can say? There are few but many sometimes forget their best resolutions; but there is this in mere good intention; that it will generally come right in the long run. Negligence may overlook, or ignorance may mistake, or zeal or resentment may overstep the proper boundary; but candor is ever ready to repair an injury or to retrace any other erroneous step.

All who know me, must be aware, that any paper in which I have any concern, must support to the utmost, by all proper means, the interests of the Troup party. The elements of the strength of that party, besides its numerical force, are to be found, it is believed, in the soundness of its doctrines; in the intelligence of its members; and especially in the concentrated unanimity of its actions. To which must be added, if not sufficiently implied already, the purity of its purposes, for to abuse the confidence of its supporters would be to lose their support. The party should act in perfect union to be successful now; and it should honestly endeavor to promote the public welfare that it may continue to be powerful. "UNION FOR THE PUBLIC GOOD" would be a motto, embracing and inculcating both its policy and its duty.

I had some reluctance in commencing this chapter of egotisms, because it could hardly fail to prove as dull, as it was felt to be awkward. And because recent circumstances have allowed me little leisure for the declarations of opinions on such grave and important matters, even as briefly as the occasion permitted. But it was due to those who honestly dissent from them wholly or partially; for many of whom, the writer entertains a high personal respect. And it was especially due to those who believe them to be sound and wholesome opinions; and to whose political cooperation and personal kindness we naturally look for support—The utter inexperience in this new avocation recounts in part for the unaffected diffidence with which he *enters upon its duties, and will entitle him, it is hoped, to some indulgence in the early part, at least, of his progress. He professes good intentions—but all profess them. He promises his best endeavors—but such promises are as plenty as blackberries. The public must, and will be the judge, whether this profession and this promise shall have been fulfilled; and so it is superfluous for the writer to invoke its decision—He sagely thinks, however, that a very extensive vote should be taken on the point and just hints to the reader of the present article, that by taking the paper, he will have the better opportunity of making up his judgment on this interesting matter.*

Its office located at the corner of Wayne and Hancock streets, the *Georgia Journal* was published twice weekly during the late fall and early winter sessions of the state legislature. The paper did not profit from its subscription rates ($3.00 per year if paid in advance, otherwise $4.00) but from its numerous advertisements. Although the *Journal* of necessity published the prosaic, repetitious yet lucrative advertisements, the sure touch of the hand of its new editor was evident throughout the paper. Here, printed between columns devoted to the political issues of the day, Prince's own editorials on the "obnoxious" tariff and the pros and cons of nullification, can be found many stories indicating his literary taste.

Racy and slightly irreverent, "The Fair Penitent," published in the *Journal* in 1832, displayed a surprise ending, preceding by many years the famed O. Henry stories. Prince's appreciation for satire could be seen in his choice of "The Petticoat Parliament." Published in July 1832, it told the exquisitely ironic tale of an English parliament composed exclusively of women members who passed many satirical and unlikely laws. And "The Militia Company Drill," the story for which the new editor became best known, was not overlooked. On November 12, 1832, it too was printed in a perhaps hard-to-fill space.

Following a contemporary practice, advertisements of proposed newspapers were often printed in Prince's *Georgia Journal*. On April 18, 1833, and in five subsequent issues, the prospectus of *The Hickory Nut and Upson Vigil* of Thomaston, Georgia, offered readers a chance to subscribe to a paper which had for its motto "Crack it who may, it will be discovered to be sound to the kernel."

The antics of the Georgia legislature did not escape Prince's notice. On February 26, 1834, he offered a free one-year subscription to the *Georgia Journal* to anyone writing on the ludicrousness of the current legislature. Although the paper in January 1833 had been awarded the coveted contract as state printer, Prince could not resist an occasional thrust at the ponderous legislature.

The pages of the *Georgia Journal*, like its competitors, were filled with political controversy. One subject, however, all agreed upon—the attempts of the state of Georgia to remove the Indians from its territory.

To achieve this end, the Georgia legislature enacted several laws, one of which was an act passed in December 1830 making it illegal for white persons to reside in Cherokee territory without having taken an oath of allegiance to the state and without a license from state authorities.

At this time white missionaries were living in north Georgia Cherokee territory, ostensibly to teach Christianity to the Indians, but suspected of interfering in political matters and encouraging the Indians to resist the state's efforts to remove them. In 1831, two of these missionaries were arrested for illegal residency and sentenced to four years of hard labor in the state penitentiary at Milledgeville.

From Augusta, David Buel, who was the husband of Oliver's first cousin Harriet Hillhouse, wrote a congratulatory letter to Prince. David, a prominent judge in Troy who added "Jun" after his signature to differentiate himself from the senior Buel, expressed his opinion on the Indian proceedings in Georgia:

Oliver H. Prince, Esq.   Augusta, March 17th 1832

Dear Sir, I am thus far on my way from Florida and as our cousin, D. P. Hillhouse who came here yesterday, says he gave you to understand I should pass through Milledgeville, I deem it my duty to write to correct his mistake. I have never anticipated that pleasure, gratifying as it would have been.

My plan is to go to Washington on Monday, spend a few days with our friends there & then go homeward in the stage—

I take this occasion to congratulate you upon your promotion from the Lawyers office to the Editors Closet with the prospect (as I hear) of improvement on the score of finances—and that I should think without an increase of toil—I was sorry to meet in Savannah the decision of the Supreme Court in the case of the missionaries—Thoroughly believing as I do that the Supreme Court or some tribunal is good, and essential to the continuance of our government, I cannot but deeply deplore the ultimate consequences which I fear will flow from this decision; for I hear it said all around me that Georgia will not submit to the decision. I hear this said by men of all grades—but I hope rather than expect they are mistaken. It is not that I fear any attempt at coercion or enforcing the decision with bayonets or as your friend Judge Clayton expresses it by making Georgia a Howling Wilderness—I look not for any such events.

My apprehensions arise from the inevitable altho' slower consequences of having a decision made by our Sup. Court which will be disregarded by a Respectable member of our Confederacy—I would that Georgia pride had a somewhat different direction—that it would be her pride to give effect to the decision by letting those poor missionaries go as Sterne's LeFever did the fly, telling him the world was wide enough for both.—I do not approve the conduct of the missionaries. They did not in my judgment act in the Spirit of our Saviour when they refused to quit the territory or take the oath, even admitting it had been certain that the laws of Georgia were unconstitutional. And much less do I approve the answer taken by the Employers & friends, political and religious, of the missionaries at the North & East. I consider it mainly owing to the injudicious interference of the professed friends of the Cherokees that the tribe is not now quietly enjoying the protection of the General government beyond the Mississippi. You well know my opinion on this subject I need not therefore enlarge— nor have I any hesitation to say that until this decision was made I have supposed the question whether Georgia should extend her laws over the Cherokees was altogether a question of morals between her & the Indians—and I did not perceive any unconstitutionality in those laws. For as I understood our history, it had been the practice of the States while colonies & since to govern Indians within their bounds & when they deemed proper, to subject them to their laws. These opinions I have held and maintained not without some censure among the Philo' Cherokees at the north.

I have not seen the reasons assigned by the Court for the opinion which they have given, but if the reasons assigned should not be convincing; the decision itself is nevertheless entitled to respect as the judgment of the tribunal constituted to expound the laws—and to decide on the question of constitutionality of laws made by State governments at least, educated as I have been I think if I were now even a Georgian I should feel bound by the decision for the simple reason that I am as a citizen of the U.S. bound by its Constitution; and the Supr. Court derives from the Constitution & the laws made by Congress power to decide in the last. I know that some say the Court had not jurisdiction, but it appears to me that when a Citizen of the U.S. has his rights affected by the judgment of a State Court, he has the right to test the constitutionality of the law in the Supreme Court of the U.S. Such at any rate has been the practice from the beginning and the State of New Hampshire, New York, Pennsylvania & others have had their laws declared void and submitted to the decisions—But pardon my running on this subject. I cannot expect that any opinions of mine will have any influence & therefore I dismiss it with expressing the hope that the Evil which I fear will not happen— and that the Almighty may long, very long, preserve our happy government from dissolution—Genl. Jackson never expressed a more important sentiment than the one devoted against the nullifiers "The Union must be preserved."

I expect to be at Washington, Geo a week or more and shall be happy, if your leisure permits, to get a line from you letting me know how all do. My letters from home are to 3 instant. Wife and family were in tolerable health.

My health the past winter has been quite comfortable. I am suffering more now by the late sudden change of the weather than I have anytime during the winter. I found St. Augustine quite a delightful climate—

I learn from Cousin David that he was <u>Reformed</u> out of his office of legislation by your new Executive in a rather unceremonious manner. But you Georgians have an original way of doing up your matters. Cousin Lucy I hear is quite rejoiced that her husband is permitted to return to domestic endeavorments—Cousin D. intimated that Cousin Lucy now begins to talk of another trip to the north which I perceive Cousin David does not entirely relish. He seems of opinion that Washington is quite a pleasant & desirable residence.

Please to remember me specially to Mrs. Prince, Oliver & the little girls.

> *I am very sincerely your friend*
> *David Buel Jun*

Later in the month Thomas Hillhouse, Prince's uncle, wrote his nephew a long letter in which he, too, refers to the Cherokee controversy.

Dear Nephew,   *Albany, March 26th 1832*
  Your letter of the 3d ult. was duly rece'd although I have delayed acknowledging it to this time. I find nothing to interest you in the telling except that "we are all well & hope these fine lines will find you So"—we are now at the close of a long cold old fashioned winter & which has well sustained it's character to the end in the breaking up of our river, reminding <u>old folks</u> of former years & perhaps gratifying some of them that their predictions of danger from approaching with modern improvements nearer to the line or range of danger from the overflow of water & ice is now been verified. Without undertaking to give particulars (for which see papers) will only say that the rise of water was greater than ever before known & with the floating ice has done much damage. The ice damned & stopped a little above Albany, so that the flood was greater here & at Troy than therein, it has scraped off most of the fences on the flatts, of course ours with the rest. Your friend Judge Clayton I think has done himself much credit in the affair of the U.S. Bank. I hope the Committee appointed to investigate its affairs will make a thorough inquiry notwithstanding all the impediments that will probably be thrown in their way. You will recollect that some 10 or 12 years past a like Committee was sent on to Philadelphia of which our John C. Spencer was Chairman, their report was very full & fully supported most of the charges made against the institution besides new discoveries. At all events I think this Committee in their report will show enough to prevent the renewal of their Charter unless with very important modifications.
  As to your removal to Milledgeville & new undertaking I can say nothing on the score of profit & loss, this much however, is gratifying that you are Sixty miles more or less

nearer to us & which would be still more pleasing were it 600—it may be superfluous to say that you have all our good wishes for its success.

There is now a prospect of my visiting Georgia provided you do not submit to the decision of the Supreme Court, an army of Yankees will be sent to compel you to release those <u>two worthy missionaries</u> which you have immured in your Penitentiary for disobeying the laws of your State & for their <u>laudible zeal</u> & <u>labours</u> to benefit your independent Nation of Cherokees; as I am rather old to exercise the military art I think I shall electioneer for an appointment in [the] Commissary department, but more of this when I arrive in hostile array to furnish supplies of Hog meat & hommony or to levy contributions.

We have not heard from Montville since last November. Your Uncle Samuel was then mostly confined to his bed or room with his unyielding complaint. Our friends at N. Haven by last news from them were well—Our three Boys are still at the Quaker School at Chatham. Your Aunt & S. Ann wishes an affectionate Salutation to you & Cousin Mary.

> & I am as ever your affectionate
> Uncle
> Tho' Hillhouse

NB   Since closing this morning Ten Broeck & wife who are now here say their best love & wishes must be sent to you & Cousin Mary—Weather this day—morning rain turned to snow storm—how is it with you—

In August of 1832, Oliver Prince's Milledgeville journal noted "Expenses to Athens, $20.00." A trustee of the University of Georgia, or Franklin College as it was called at the time, he had promised *Georgia Journal* readers that he would not adhere strictly to "the political strifes of the day but will strive to publish the lighter side of life for in doing so we experience a personal pleasure in making selections for these purposes."

In a letter dated August 2, 1832, and published shortly thereafter, Prince in his usual light, bantering style gave his newspaper readers a word picture of commencement week at Athens.

Why should we be always grave? We must not wear ourselves and readers out with incessant hard politics; for politics in these days are hard enough in good truth. We must all relax a little occasionally, if only to keep off the Cholera, which is frightened away, they say, by a laugh, as wolves are by a fire. The following letter has the merit of cheerfulness at least; and may not be unacceptable to some of our readers, as a gleam of sunshine in this "winter of our discontent."

Athens, August 2d 1832

You see by my date that I am here, though it were melancholy to relate how I got here to be "knocked into a cocked hat" is highly figurative, to be squeezed into every other shape is not perhaps as entertaining to the fancy, but if you will pardon the pun, I think it makes fully as deep an impression. Beautiful Athens! beautiful in thy bowers; thy green-grass plats; thy neat white houses embosomed in trees; thy high situation elevated for prospect, air and health; and pleasant above all, in thy hospitable intelligent society! Thyself in the bloom of youth, art already the nurse of Genius; now fostering its energies, now training its growth in either the severe or tasteful sciences! Rural, shady, cheerful, classic village! Opulent in resources! Rich in promise! My corporeal man may be cramped in thy annual crowds, but my spirit is at home in thy halls, and loves to meet its ever ready welcome at thy thresholds—but enough. You see I'm inspired and what more would you have?

To come down to a plain question in plain prose, did you

ever lodge five in a bed with the floor full besides? I will not say I have done it; but to live in the constant fear of such a catastrophe, is in some degree to endure it. The wealthy residents of the place ought to render to the public the service of taking boarders during commencement. Their motive would be universally understood as promoting the good of the institution and of the town and the accommodation of their friends and not for any purpose of emolument. The attendence here would perhaps be double, if comfortable accommodations could be conveniently procured. The four or five public houses take all they can, and more than they ought; and they do as well by their guests as perhaps is possible in such an overwhelming crowd. But after the best they can do, one week of such cram and jam must often deter the guest from a second visit.

There are twenty odd reasons why the college edifices ought to be in good taste; the only one of which reasons I shall now mention is, that it is much more useful and costs no more, to lay a brick in one position than it does in another. The old college stands well, considering it was built by the lowest bidder. Few buildings have a good constitution that are born under the auspices of an auctioneer's hammer; they generally sink into an early decline—But the new college! When Soloman wrote of there being nothing new under the Sun, he had not seen this said college; and so its appearance does no discredit to the wisdom of that wisest of men—Having a full cornice on one side and none on the other; the gable suggests the idea of a jockey cap with its brim in front. The whole external surface of the walls is plastered; and an awkward attempt to paint them like blocks of marble or free stone presents the lively resemblance of a harlequin's jacket, or more nearly perhaps, that of a patch-work of boiled tripe! What would Soloman say of that if he could now publish a new edition of his proverbs?

The new chapel is externally a good imitation of grey granite and is a fine model of Grecian architecture. Plain, chaste, and as far as I can judge, the building and the doric colonade in front are in just proportions. The seats and gallery within will contain perhaps a thousand or twelve hundred persons; and when filled, as it was on each day of the exercises, presents a spectacle gratifying alike to almost every sense and every proper sentiment. The centre part of the spacious area, densely filled with female beauty, taste and fashion, bordered all round by a mass equally close of the other sex, seemed like an agriette of brilliant gems, in some graver, but strong and costly setting. Perfumes filled the breathing atmosphere, music stole upon the ear, smiling faces, and every variety of tasteful costume met the eye; and education the guardian genius of public liberty and private happiness seemed to preside and to shed its bright and cheerful influence over and throughout the whole. The economy of society is not capable, I think, of presenting any scene of such high and chastened rational and various pleasure, as is annually exhibited in this now well conducted seminary.

The orations as you know were all original, the delivery, generally good, sometimes fine. Very little of the chanting cadence, once so prevalent that I have thought I could distinguish by a young man's tune of oratory in what college he had been educated; each seminary having its own peculiar tune. Young men are apt to emphasize with their knees, and all young persons speak too fast; but no man speaks slow till he becomes self collected. I noticed with pleasure that the seniors had profited in this respect by their exercises. They were less hurried than the juniors. The oration pronounced on Thursday before the two societies, by Mr. Nesbit of the Demostheneans, was a fine production. Rich perhaps to redundancy in classical allusion, full of happy and original conceptions and delivered in that calm clear *collectedness of manner that characterizes the style of that gentleman's oratory. For*

> *"When he speaks, what elocution flows!*
> *Like the soft fleeces of descending snows."*

On Wednesday night there was a grand ball. I was also told of a tragedy to be played at the Theatre, and was well disposed to go, and purchase a dollars worth of grief; being myself somewhat unprovided with the article; but I acquiesced in the preference of some of my company, and we attended a concert in the new chapel of vocal and instrumental music which they called an oratorio. Learning on enquiry, that I was not obliged to listen to any more of it then I chose, I consulted my pleasure in that respect and attended to but little of it. Some that I did hear was very fine, as I was told on good authority. It was evidently difficult. You must look at the fiddler's fingers to find the merit which distinguishes modern scientific harmony—mind I say nothing of melody—from that natural genuine music, which reaches and moves the heart. There was the proper quantity, I suppose, of sudden stops & breaks and catches and snatches. There were terrific rumblings of the thoroughbass and dreadful hard sawings of cat-gut equally base, and thereupon an instant transition to the finis spun quivering quidling diddle-de-dee, that made it manifest at once, what a difference there essentially is between thunder and squeak. I think I begin to understand it. The first part of the process is intended to begin at the foundation and stir up the soul of the inner man from its very bottom as it were; and then comes the diddling part, with divers affecting flourishes of the fiddle bow, duly to tickle his upper part into a proper condition, and the thing is done—the feat is performed, the man is happy all over from his head to his heel; and this is all he needs to know of the matter. He might indeed find great delight in the technicals, some of which I have occasionally over heard; such as the dominants and sub-dominants, the intervals and simple intervals; the diapason the semi-tones, dis-tones, tria-tones and all the other tones. He might cultivate an agreeable acquaintance with the third, fourth and fifth and the rest of the majors; and talk learnedly of a syncopation of the fundamental bass. All this may afford real pleasure no doubt; but it is the pleasure of pedantry, not of music, with which it has about as much connection as a fox chase has with algebra or acoustics.

I would not ride with Swift fifty miles to see a man who was pleased he knew not why, and laughed he cared not wherefore; but I would like to be that very man. You must not accuse me of misspelling my signature; I do not intend to write the name of either of the Cleans of old, but I intend just what I write,

CLEUN

News was received in 1833 that Oliver's uncle William Hillhouse had died in New Haven, Connecticut. Since he had died intestate and had never married, the Georgia relatives were apparently to inherit a share of his large property holdings in New York and elsewhere. Prince wrote a lengthy letter of attorney, naming his uncle Thomas Hillhouse and cousin Judge Buel as representatives of the family interests. In addition to Prince, the Georgia relatives were David Porter Hillhouse, his sister Mary Hillhouse Shepherd, and Adam L. Alexander (husband of Sarah Hillhouse Gilbert Alexander).

From Washington, Prince heard again from David Porter Hillhouse, who wrote to ask his cousin Oliver to insert a notice in the *Georgia Journal* advertising the sale of his colts. Newspapers in the state were giving much space to news of states' rights meetings, and David expressed his views on some of the political figures on the scene in 1834.

Dear Sir,   *Washington, 6th February 1834*

In the "News" of this date, you will observe an advertisement (which I have directed the printers to mark for your paper) concerning my horse Quidnunc. As you seem to have departed from your former rule, by having lately inserted such notices in your "Journal", I desire you to publish the advertisement I have referred to <u>once conspicuously</u> in the Georgia Journal and oblige me by making a personal request for it's <u>conspicuous</u> insertion once in the Recorder and in the Federal Union. If they will not publish the whole advertisement, ask them to copy so much as relates to the character of the horse's colts, and the premiums proposed for the best of them.

You will see by the "News" that we have had our state rights' meeting, and that I am mis-placed at the head of the association. This ought not to have been done, but cannot now be remedied. Chandler's speech on the occasion was very spirited, and in many parts deeply eloquent. Toombs would have <u>come out</u> in the best style, but for the unfortunate occurrence of his brother's death a few days before.

We shall have a desperate struggle from this time til October. It looks ahead to me like a long, hot, parching summer.

I do not understand the allusion that is made in some of the papers to a probable vacancy in the State rights ticket for Congress. Who is meant?—or who is probably meant? What freak has induced the annunciation of Grantland's name? Has he withdrawn it? for I do not see it in the <u>late</u> papers. 'Tis whispered here, he has joined the U.C.D.R. Ratifiers—is this so? I wish General Newnan would decline, and let Nesbett take his place. We could do much better, I think.

You have understood that we <u>lost</u> our county officers. It was entirely owing to the inclemency of the weather—the bad state of the roads and the unwarrantable confidence of many of our friends. But they have just aroused again, now 'tis over—and if they do not dose again before fall, I think they will tell their numbers.

If it were not for the very bad condition of the roads,
Lucy and I would try to make you a visit next month, but
they are too bad hereabouts to risk one's neck on wheels.
Our regards to Cousin Mary & Self & Chicks.

> *Your friend,*
> *D. P. Hillhouse*

O. H. Prince Esq.

In an 1834 letter to Judge Buel, Oliver Prince ordered
through his cousin twenty blinds or shutters from a New
York builder. The letter does not state the fact, but it seems
likely that he was building or had partially completed a
house in Milledgeville. Although they still maintained a
home in Macon the Princes, according to Oliver's journal,
paid $44.00 a month for board in Milledgeville to Mrs.
Godwin. But Prince had always lived well, and surely he
wanted a home in Milledgeville for his family. Also eleven-
year-old Oliver Jr.'s education was very much on his father's mind. The letter reflects Prince's current concerns.

My Dear Sir,   *July 15th 1834*
I really think it is not much to the credit of either of us,
that we hear so seldom—so very seldom, from each other. I
suspect however the cause is very much the same with you
as with me. I have much of business, important & unim-
portant. So many cares, great & little, on my mind. So many
letters on my hands that I must *write, that I postpone my*
own enjoyments, so repeatedly from time to time, till all
the little procrastinations put together make out a great
amount. Uncle Thomas writes to me every 5 or 6 months
and, I, taking about half that time to answer him, we inter-
change intelligence *or communication about as often prob-*
ably as London does with Bombay or Calcutta. I hear from
you generally through him as far as a general remark that
"all are well" or the like.

To bring this letter a little more within the established habit that we seem both to have fallen into I even connect it with a matter of business. I suppose it would seem still more "<u>Naytural</u>" as Maj. Downing or the Stricklands would say if it was to be accompanied with a fee; but it happens to be all the other way—all the trouble to you and the accruing benefit to me.

The enclosed letter will explain itself. If I am not overdrawing on your kindness to request your attention to it, I must ask you to deliver it to Ayres & Thayer, and if it be not too much trouble be the medium of their communication to me. To make them perfectly sure & easy as to their pay, I have ventured to name you as my Banker again. Can I place you in funds by a draft on N. York? It would be inconvenient to procure one on Troy or Albany. I have recommended Mr. A & T's work to several of my friends, one of whom (Mr. Cole) wrote to me from Macon for their address, intending as he said to send an order, whether he ever did so I never thought to inquire.

R. K. Hines, Esq. who is now building a house here adopts my suggestion and intends to get his shutters he says from A & T. I told them I should recommend their work & have never failed to do so.

Mary, my wife, has not enjoyed very good health of late. An obstructed perspiration seems to be the principal difficulty; so that she is generally better in warm than in cold weather. Our three children are all well, though not as robust as I could wish. I have always desired to place Oliver at a school conducted on the Fellenburg plan. You do not agree with me entirely in my approbation of that system I believe, but I am & have long been satisfied that the natural habits & tendencies of his mind is best adapted to that mode of instruction. If any such school happens to occur to your recollection (without any trouble of inquiry or reference,) please to mention it in your answer. I suppose your boys are all entirely through the classics by this time. Please let me know how they all are, and what is the state of Cousin Harriet's health.

I presume your father is still living, not having heard to the contrary, please remember us to him & remind him of the pleasant times we had in N. York. Our rambles about town, our visit to Therborn's (who I understand has turned author) and our pleasant attendance on the sermon at the Moravian Church in Fulton Street. Mrs. Prince has good hopes with good luck to see him again, & she bespeaks him as her escort before any person else. My health has in general been excellent & they flatter me by telling me that I seem to grow younger. An old gentleman on being introduced to me the other day, remarked that many years ago he knew my father who then practiced law & attended Oglethorpe Court. This <u>father</u>, you understand, was myself.

We are particularly desirous of learning how your health is of late. Do you intend to come South again? If so will Georgia be out of your route? Be assured we should rejoice to see you. Once more, remember Mary & myself most affectionately to all

Yours truly
O. H. Prince

Before Judge Buel received Prince's July 15 letter, he wrote to inform him of the death of yet another uncle, Thomas Hillhouse.

Oliver H. Prince Esq.   *Troy, N.Y., July 20th 1834*
Dear Sir,

It is long since we have had any direct communication with you, and it is painful to be called on to make my letter the courier of sorrowful tidings. Your Uncle Thomas Hillhouse has finished his earthly career. He left the world on Tuesday the 15th June which time numerous & pressing engagements have prevented me from writing. He was sick about four weeks I do not know that the primary seat of his

disease is perfectly ascertained. His liver had been affected
in the previous winter and there was some affliction of the
heart. But in the progress of his disease it appeared the
form of obstinate dropsy in the limbs progressing until it
reached the body. He seemed sensible during his sickness
that his end approached—and spoke with calmness of his
expected decease. His death is extensively lamented. He
was greatly respected by a numerous circle in the neigh-
borhood including Albany and Troy. His remains are de-
posited in a new stone vault or rather tomb which he had
constructed several years since in a family Cemetery about
thirty rods from his house·across the meadow on the side
of the hill—It is constructed of strong masonry & sur-
rounded by trees & running vines. He spoke with much
satisfaction of having prepared such a spot to place his
body in—during his illness. I know that the information of
his death will be sad tidings to you for you were acquainted
with his amiable and useful traits of character. It did seem
until his last sickness that his frame was one which would
have borne the march of time many years longer. His young
and interesting family are deprived of a most important
friend. His oldest son, Thomas, gives promise of being a
useful, industrious and respectable man, the other boys are
too young to develop their characters. The Elder branches
of the Hillhouse family are now almost extinct. Your Uncle
Samuel remains—but entirely helpless.

We have with us our good friend and Cousin, Mrs. Shep-
herd, her two daughters Charlotte & Caroline & her youn-
gest son Heywood—Mrs. Shepherd has been to Hadley to
visit her mothers connections & returned here just in time
to attend the funeral of Uncle Thomas—She designed to
leave Heywood & Caroline at school at the north and will
with Charlotte return to the South by land about the 1st of
October.

I have occasionally heard of you & Mrs. Prince through

Uncle Thomas—We should be glad when you feel so inclined to hear directly from you—My recollections of Georgia are vivid and my attachments to my friends there unabated— Since my last return from the South my health has been continually improving. For the last year I have performed as much hard professional labour as in any year of my life without any detriment to my health. I, however, continue my vegetable diet & probably shall do so all my life as it seems to be especially adapted to my constitution.

Mrs. Alexander has been in New York & New Haven several weeks, she is now expecting her husband on, and I believe they intend to make us a call on their way to Saratoga.

Did Mrs. Prince get satisfied with the North so as to feel no inclination to revisit us? Has Mrs. Prince ever become acquainted with the Reverend Bragg, the Episcopal minister at Macon? He is we think a man of great excellence of character and I should be gratified to have him make your acquaintance as I reckon him among my particular friends. Is Oliver learning Greek & Latin? Tell him his Cousin Samuel has got thro' his college course and is now a tutor at Kenyon College, Ohio—David Hillhouse & John Griswold are at Bristol College 20 miles above Philadelphia on the Banks of the Delaware—At this college the Students work on the farm or in the Mechanic Shops 3 hours a day & study the residue of the time—This is the place at which Mrs. Shepherd intends to leave Heywood.

Mrs. Buel desires to be affectionately remembered to Mrs. Prince—

> *With great Esteem I am*
> *Affectionately yours*
> *David Buel Jun*

On August 5, Judge Buel answered Oliver's letter of July 15, complying with his request of a quote on window blinds and recommendation of a school for Oliver Jr.

O. H. Prince Esq   Troy, August 5th 1834
Dear Sir

Your letter bearing date the 15th July was received during my absence from home. On my return I attended to your request & have today received Mr. Thayers proposition—Mr. Ayres & he are not now in partnership—His calculation & proposition is as follows "I propose to furnish blinds for 20 windows of the size & description wanted by O. H. Prince Esq painted complete for $3.75 each–$75.00

4 pairs 6 inch parliament hinges 1/9	2.88
3 Doz. pair 3 ½ by 3 Inch. . . . . . . 16/.	6.00
3 ½ gross screws 6/	0.50
20 Setts Millers fastenings	6.80
Boxing Cartage & freight to New York	5.00
	21.18
	96.18

He ultimately concluded to call the whole amount $95— which brings the Blinds with trimmings & del[d] in N.Y. at $4.75 a window.

Mr. Thayer will agree to deliver them in N. York in 5 weeks after he receives direction to make them. If you decide to have him do the job you will of course let me know on receipt of this—It will give me great pleasure to the matter of business tho "not accompanied with a fee"—

In respect to a School—I know of one which I think so highly of that I have two boys, Hillhouse & John at it & Mrs. Shepherd's youngest boy Haywood has enrolled there at the opening of the fall term 1st October. It is situated on the Banks of the Delaware 18 miles above Philadelphia & 3 miles south of Bristol on the Pennsylvania side. The Institution has, I believe, as much of Fellenburg in it as is wanted. The younger boys work 2 hours a day & the older ones three, either on the farm or in the workshops—Hillhouse works at the Carpenters trade & has learned to use the broad axe,

plane and with considerable skill & to the advantage of his
health. John is a "tiller of the ground" & has the reputation
of being a good "workey." The Institution is a society by itself
excluded from the world & under strict paternal discipline.

It is incorporated & consists of 1—A Select Elementary
School limited to 25 scholars—2—An Academical or fitting
department 3—A college arranged into the usual College
Classes. The whole is under the same President & faculty. I
attended the commencement a fortnight since & was much
gratified—The Institution is under direction of Episcopa-
lians. The Rev. Chauncy Colton is President, Lieut Pendleton,
educated at West point & late of the Army, is the Mathemati-
cal professor, the other professor-ships are well filled. Hillhouse now enters in his junior year & John his Sophomore.
It is a new Institution, there are in all about 80 Students.
The Expense for a year in the select department (exclusive of
Clothes & Books) is abt $200. If you wish more information
about it I would refer you to Rev. Stephen Tyng of Philadelphia or Rev. G. W. Ridgely, Bristol, Pa. The situation is one
of great beauty & I believe very healthful.

As I have had occasion recently to write to you as to the
death of Uncle Thomas Hillhouse I will close my communication with the request to be particularly remembered to Mrs.
Prince in which request my wife unites. Mrs. Shepherd & 3
children are with us. I think Mrs. S. enjoys her visit to the
north. My own health is good—I trust I shall not for healths
sake be compelled to immigrate south but it would if I could
conveniently leave home gratify me to visit Georgia.

I am truly your friend
David Buel, Jun

As you ask about my boys I might add that Samuel was
graduated about a year since at Williamstown where he took a
high standing and soon after being graduated he went to
Kenyon College in the State of Ohio and was appointed a tutor in that institution. We expect him home on a visit soon.

Oliver Prince's newspaper was prospering. He and his partner Thomas Ragland soon were looking for a young man who could help them in the difficult task of printing a newspaper. They found such a boy in Green Mitchell Culverhouse, who was indentured to them in April 1835.

On January 13, 1835, the *Georgia Journal* printed a letter supposedly from a student of the law school at Augusta. But very likely it was written by Prince himself and may provide a clue as to how he attained his mastery of the law profession. An excerpt reads:

Our school comes on bravely. . . . The peculiar propriety, observed in the arrangement and order of the several titles—the <u>rules</u> as applicable to Georgia practice and Legislation: together with the fact, that we generally read some elementary author on the subject upon which he (Gould) is lecturing hearing the lecture, and taking it down at the time, in a brief form—retiring to our rooms, and carefully writing it down at length, as though they were to be <u>printed</u>—on Saturday morning, after the lecture, an attentive reading of the past weeks labor, preparatory to examination in the evening, all tend, in the most eminent degree, to fix the attention and assist the memory. I can say this (at least for myself) that I have learned more since my arrival here, than I should have done in <u>two</u> years in a Lawyer's office, with the scanty attention generally paid to the students by their preceptors. These Lectures have greatly improved my memory, and especially the faculty of <u>close attention</u>. I have not read the elementary authors as much as some of the others; but, on the contrary have bestowed my whole attention upon the <u>Lectures themselves</u>, carefully studying and <u>digesting</u>, and writing down in <u>my own</u> language, all the <u>rules</u> and <u>principles</u> of each title in succession; (and you may take my word for it, that the <u>thorough</u> mastery and comprehension of these, were fully sufficient

for the time) The consequence is, that at our examina-
tions, (having studied the <u>principles</u> well) I can always an-
swer a question <u>readily in my own way</u>—if not in the pre-
cise language of the Rule. I have not missed 5 questions
since I have been here. While, on the other hand, some of
our students particularly —— and —— seem wholly am-
bitious of keeping <u>ahead with their lectures</u> whether <u>they</u>
<u>understand them or not.</u> This is folly. And they feel the
effects on examination. They are <u>labouring hard</u>; but are
actually profiting <u>less</u>, less than myself—though I have
<u>read</u> and <u>written</u> a great deal <u>less</u>. The secret is, I don't rest
until I <u>comprehend</u> everything I have to <u>copy</u>. I am now
imbibing knowledge, almost <u>intuitively</u>.

The *Georgia Journal* apparently was read in cities other
than Milledgeville, for a responding letter from Augusta
arrived, signed "A Member of The Law School." The writer
severely upbraided Prince for printing the letter, and even
questioned its authenticity. Prince was so delighted with the
whole affair that he made a copy of the scolding letter and
printed it in the *Journal*'s equivalent of the "Letters to the
Editor" columns.

In April 1835, Prince wrote to David Buel requesting a
letter of attorney and representation in the legal matter of
his Uncle William Hillhouse's estate.

Dear Sir   Milledgeville, 13 April 1835
I have accepted Cousin Saml Hillhouse's proposition to
pay me for my share of Uncle William Hillhouse's estate,
"$2000 on delivery of the deed" I must ask you to repre-
sent me in making the title & the receipt of the money. Will
you have the goodness to send a letter of attorney for me to
execute for that purpose? I would not think of putting you
to that trouble, but for the obvious purpose of avoiding all
error or informality—I would request Mr. Baldwin to do it,

but as he resides in another state, he may not be perfectly familiar with the requirements in New York where it is to be executed or acted on.

We are all in the enjoyments of our usual health. We still board at a boarding house, but shall resume housekeeping after next year.

We seldom hear from you, but you and yours are often the subject of our conversations. We have already lived over again four times (as the seasons recur) the pleasant time we spent in Troy, and if we should never see Mount Ida again the rides & walks & talks & sittings will long form a sunny bright spot in the morning of the past. Feeling thus, it would seem downright sentimental if I was to attempt to tell you how much pleasure I felt in the hope you so kindly expressed of seeing us again at Troy. Of course I know not whether an event so important to us in the even tenor of our methodical life will ever happen, but I can assure you I hope it may. To dismiss the idea would be very painful. The happy restoration of your health which you well deserve & which I suppose none but such system, method & perseverance as yours could have accomplished—this return of your health I suppose excludes the idea of your again seeing Georgia.

I wish I had some business that rendered it <u>necessary</u> for me to go to England. It is to me a mortifying reflection that I am to take leave of this globe of earth, never having seen but one side of it, particularly that now to go to Liverpool is so much like merely crossing a ferry. Your father, I presume is as happy & cheerful as ever, as it is constitutional. But he cannot be as active as when we saw him, a failure in this respect must be constitutional also. I must present Mary's love to Cousin Harriet before I do my own. I know not which is greatest but the ladies . . . [this part of letter missing] *. . . and servants too. Pray remember us to them each & individually. I know we ought not to bear malice*

Rockwell, Milledgeville.

*against them. If they are so much smarter than ours, they
could hardly help it, poor things—the fault is mainly with
their haunts. Once more, our kindest remembrances.*

O. H. P.

As the letter indicates, the Princes's dream of owning
their own home had not been cast aside. They had recently
been visited by J. H. Lloyd, who had lent Prince a portfolio
of architectural drawings. A letter from Lloyd, preserved
by Virginia Prince for its words of praise for her scholarship, shows that Oliver Prince had been consulting that
book of architectural plans.

Dear Sir

*Mrs. Tanner of Columbus, Aunt to Mrs. Lloyd will prob-
ably deliver this to you, if so, I should feel myself obliged
by your giving her the Port-folio of Architectural Drawings
I left in your care and may I beg the favour of you having it
so secured by the Cloth around it, as to fit it for the ups and
downs it is likely to receive.*

*I sometimes since wrote to Mr. Deane desiring him to
present our respects to Mrs. Prince yourself and family, I
have received no answer to my letter therefore know not
whether he fulfilled my request, but whether he did or not,
I hope you will believe my Wife and I will ever feel grateful
for the polite attention we experienced from Mrs. Prince
and yourself during our short sojourn at Milledgeville.*

*We are much pleased with Columbus but not having yet
fully determined upon my ultimate plans, I will defer trou-
bling you with a long letter until I shall be enabled to write
more fully.*

*Mrs. Lloyd now joins me in respectful regards to Mrs.
Prince and yourself and beg you to present our love to
your family. I hope Virginia still studies her French lessons,
please to say to her, I would be very glad to have her here*

to place before some of my pupils as an example of good conduct and scholarship, indeed I may with truth spare you Sir; I should feel proud to point to her as one of my scholars.

I will not at present take up your valuable time longer than to entreat you to excuse the trouble I am giving you and to beg you to believe

> *I am with great esteem*
> *Dear Sir*
> *Your most obedient servant*
> *J. H. Lloyd*
> *Columbus, 18 June 1835*

To
O. H. Prince Esq.

Prince's son, Oliver Jr., in spite of some letters written to the Hillhouse relatives for advice on schooling for him, had been enrolled at Midway Boys Preparatory Academy near Milledgeville. From the many entries of "Shoes for Oliver" in Prince Sr.'s journals, it was apparent that Oliver Jr. was still rough on shoes. In one of the son's letters to his father, Prince underlined the misspelled words used by the twelve-year-old.

Dear father   *Midway, August 23d 1835*
I now take the opportunity of writing to you. Having received yours I now sit down to answer it. Mr. Beman told me that you said I must come in Saturday but one of my feet was very sore so that I could hardly walk. Saturday at <u>diner</u> *I was not very well and I threw up all of my* <u>diner</u>. *I wish that you would (send) me a toilet-glass one of the most common kind for I have* <u>unluckedly</u> *broke one of my companions, and I wish also that you would [send] me my shoes which are in our room for my others have worn out. I wish to see you all very much and I wish that you and mother*

*would ride out here some evening and see me. Give my
love to mother and the children.*

Your affectionate son

Among Prince's manuscripts is one that at first defied in-
terpretation. It was written in a bold, careless hand in the
form of a letter to his newspaper, with many word changes
and strike-throughs. It told the interesting story of an old
bureau bought at an auction which contained ancient manuscripts. The story, entitled "Empire of Harumscambia,"
was probably never rewritten to Prince's satisfaction, and
so remains, like many of his other writings, unrecorded.

Men of Mark in Georgia called Oliver Hillhouse Prince a
"literary man," but most of his work as a writer is not trace-
able. Some publishings of the period appeared anonymously, as newspaper editors often wrote short, humorous
"fillers" and printed them in their respective papers under
pseudonyms. But one short story remains a classic. The
sketch was entitled "The Militia Company Drill" and was
published in Augustus Baldwin Longstreet's book, *Georgia
Scenes*, in 1835.

Longstreet, a lawyer from Augusta, had been elected to
the state legislature in 1821. During his term in Milledgeville, Prince's *Digest of the Laws of the State of Georgia* was
printed, and it is probable that the two had met there.
From January 1834 until July 1836, Judge Longstreet published a newspaper, the *States Rights Sentinel*, in Augusta. In
April 1834, the newspaper began publishing installments
of "Georgia Scenes, By a Native Georgian." The sketches
were signed "Hall" or "Baldwin," yet everyone knew the
author was Longstreet.

One story, however, bore the name "Timothy Crabshaw."
Of this sketch, "The Militia Company Drill," Longstreet
stated in a footnote that it was "from the pen of a friend of
whose labors I would have gladly availed myself oftener."
That friend was Oliver Hillhouse Prince.

Georgia Scenes later appeared in book form and enjoyed a wide and appreciative audience. Even the critical editor Edgar Allan Poe in the March 1836 issue of the *Southern Literary Messenger*, wrote, "The book reached us anonymously. . . . Seldom—perhaps never in our lives—have we laughed as immoderately over any book as over the one now before us." The popularity of *Georgia Scenes* continued over the years, going through various printings from 1835 to 1897, and to the present day is still being reprinted.

But "Militia Drill" had seen print long before 1835. John Donald Wade in his biography *Augustus Baldwin Longstreet* traced its history in a chapter entitled "Georgia Scenes— One by One." A furor had arisen in 1880, when Thomas Hardy published *The Trumpet Major*. The English novelist was accused of plagiarism involving the use of the story and even the dialogue of "Militia Drill." So much curiosity had been aroused that *The Trumpet Major* and *Georgia Scenes* were found in some bookstores prominently displayed side by side.

Hardy, in the preface to his 1895 edition of *The Trumpet Major*, denied the charge and said that he had used C. H. Gifford's *History of the Wars Occasioned by the French Revolution*, published in London in 1817. But Wade in his biography of Longstreet stated that "Militia Drill" was published even before then under the title "Captain Clodpole or the Oglethorpe Muster," which had been reprinted throughout the United States and in some parts of Europe.

Wade maintained that he himself had seen an even earlier copy bound into one volume with "The Way to Wealth" by Dr. Franklin (dateless) and "The Cutter, in Five Lectures upon the Art and Practice of Cutting Friends, Acquaintances and Relations" (date 1808). It was the "Militia Drill," and most likely its first appearance, but printed under the title "The Ghost of Baron Steuben or Fredonia in Arms! Being a Description of That Most Bloody Campaign, Styled the Alexandro-Caesaro-Eugenio-Frederico-

Bonapartic Campaign out Napoleonified, or a Georgia Training, In which most exquisite discipline, subordination, military knowledge, clearly exemplified and pathetically recommended to all who are convinced of the uselessness and mischief of a Standing Army."

Wade stated that in Gifford's *History of the Wars Occasioned by the French Revolution*, published in 1817 and which book Hardy said he used for *The Trumpet Major* drill scenes, can be found almost identically this same sketch presented as a satirical account of an American drill. Wade speculated that it must have been Oliver Hillhouse Prince's eight-page sketch of "The Ghost of Baron Steuben," published in 1808, that Gifford had used as *his* source. Wade said the Hardy episode "has been endlessly talked about."

Judge Richard H. Clark in his 1898 *Memoirs* devoted an entire chapter to "Georgia Scenes and the Trumpet Major," even printing "Militia Drill" and the contested scenes of *The Trumpet Major* side by side for comparison.

For almost four years Oliver Prince guided the *Georgia Journal* through the turbulent political upheavals of Georgia. But in October 1835 he relinquished the reins of the editorship of the paper to William S. Rockwell. Rockwell, a twenty-six-year-old attorney of Milledgeville, had recently edited the *Times and State Rights Advocate* in the Georgia capital. His statement, announcing that he had acquired the *Journal*, declared that the two papers would now be combined.

Prince and his partner, Thomas Ragland, issued a farewell message to their readers:

The 26th volume of the Georgia Journal has just closed, and in pursuance of the resolutions we formed four or five months ago, with a view to other pursuits, we have now disposed of the establishment. In taking leave of our friends, we have to express the acknowledgments due for the sup-

*port they have given us. We hope they have felt that in do-
ing so, they supported those principles on which depend
the stability of this government and the permanent liberty
and welfare of the people. Such at least has been our deep
conviction; and we have labored in the cause with a zeal
which nothing but such a conviction could have prompted
or sustained.*

*During the time, particularly the early part of it, which
the late Senior Editor has been in this office, the editorial
task has been arduous, difficult, and critical, perhaps beyond all precedent. The division and distraction of the Republican ranks, was such as threatened, not merely a temporary defeat, but destruction—as truth shall diffuse itself
as it is now doing; and to make their efforts soon tell in the
good old cause. It is possible that our own feeble efforts
may have had their effect, in aid of abler presses, and assisted by the lapse of time in producing this better state of
things. If so, we shall be gratified in the reflection that we
have not labored entirely in vain.*

Prince, not given to puffery, lauded the new editor of the
Journal with words of sincere encouragement and praise,
concluding with:

*To those of the "Journal" who have not taken the "Times,"
but who are pleased with rising talent, and growing
usefulness, we beg leave to commend the Journal in future.
It is heartily commended to their kind feelings, and confidently referred to their impartial judgement; with a full
persuasion that on a fair "taste of its quality", they will feel
abundant reason to continue their support.*

The communications between the Prince family in the
South and their northern relatives continued, although in-
termittently. A letter from Judge Buel in Troy came addressed to "Oliver H. Prince Esq. Milledgeville, Georgia."

But Milledgeville was lined through and readdressed "Athens, Ga." Prince had moved to the village in upper Georgia only the month before.

Oliver H. Prince Esq.   *Troy, March 28th 1836*
   Dear Sir   Without occupying much space in inquiring who is in fault or why our correspondence is so much interupted I resolve to break the silence and at least let you know how we do and ask for a return of like information— And first of ourselves. We i.e. my own family are all pretty well.—My father has not perceptibly altered since you were here—His health is excellent and I think he enjoys as much quiet happiness as fall to the lot of mortals in this world—My wife generally has good health.—Our youngest boy is now 16 months old and is quite the Pet not only of his grandpa but of all the family—Samuel is in New York pursuing his Divinity Studies in the General Seminary of the Episcopal Church—David Hillhouse is at Bristol College in Pennsylvania & will complete his college course in July.
   John <u>was</u> *there but was sent home in November for his roguing in helping make some bonfires of tar barrels on the college grounds. He was suspended for the term but I believe I shall not send him back. He gives me more trouble than all the rest have. Charlotte at present attends Mrs. Willards Seminary. Clarence is now at school & I think he gives as good indications of capacity as any of his Brothers. My wife's sister Mrs. Williams & her daughter have been with us through the winter & will remain sometime longer. We have had one breach in our family since you were here* <u>viz</u> *Old Mamy Jane our Blackwoman who died in November. She was probably over 81 years old though we had no means of ascertaining her age except from her recollection of events which took place in The Old French War. Uncle Thomas Hillhouses' widow & children are well. John & William are at Bristol. Thomas & Sarah Ann are at home &*

live a very retired life for the most part. Mr. Schuyler last year lost his two youngest children. His older children are well & Harriet Schuyler enjoys about her usual health. My Wife's mother died last Spring as you may probably have learnt. I have thus given you about all the Family News which occurs to me. We have had a perfect Russian Winter—It commenced very suddenly on the 20th November after a most delightful Autumn and has continued with unremitting severity. The snow has been from 4 to 6 feet deep in a region of several hundred miles round us for 3 months. I cannot give you a better idea of the appearance of our streets than by stating the fact that persons walking on opposite sides of the street on the sidewalks have been invisible to each other on account of the interposing mounds of snow. It is still lying in my yard as high as my picket fences & still higher in the street adjoining the sidewalks. The stages perform their Route on the ice as far as Pough-keepsie & until within a few days have as far as Sing-Sing. The excessive depth of the snow has made the Sleighing very bad most of the winter—the roads being full of pitch holes & it being very difficult to turnout on meeting other Sleighs. The sleigh paths on the ice, however, have been & are still very fine and smooth—During the severity of our weather I should have been glad if I could have taken flight to Georgia or Florida for some weeks. I have, however, been for the chief part of the Winter very well. Indeed my health for three years past has been very good and I have been able to apply myself very constantly to my Professional Labours.

I suppose now you have become an Editor you do not embark in the Collisions of the Bar. Indeed we hear so seldom about you that we hardly know whether you continue your Editorship. It would be gratifying occasionally to hear of you & yours—Mrs. Prince is affectionately remembered both by my wife and myself and I should like much to hear how young Oliver progresses in his career of fitting for the occupation of life.—We are so far advanced in our career that we must live in our children. It is therefore quite desirable to know whether they will make good our plans. I hope Master Oliver has begun to think seriously of fitting himself to fill a good large place on the world's theatre. We occasionally hear from our other Georgia Friends at Washington. It is understood that Cousin David & Lucy will visit the North the coming year. Why could not you & Mrs. Prince do the like? The steam Navigation to Norfolk & the Rail Roads on this side the Potamack have annihilated more than half the distance in time and trouble. Indeed an excursion from Georgia to New York is now attended with scarcely any risk or fatigue. Mrs. Shepherd also intends to come on this year and I believe will take Caroline home when she returns. Heywood she probably will leave at the North awhile longer. The last letter which I remember to have news from you related to the sale of your share of your Uncle Williams estate to Samuel Hillhouse. I waited a good while to hear from the Connecticutt people respecting it & learned at length that the Business was attended to at New Haven. Samuel has since purchased the shares of our side of the family & that of one of the Raymonds & has I believe contracted for the share belonging to Uncle Thomas' estate. I really hope Samuel will make something out of it—for it will be attended with immense trouble. After I ascertained the situation of the property I would hardly have undertaken to settle up the Estate for the whole of it & determined to sell out our share for what we could get—

I hope you will let us hear from you before long. We shall always retain our feelings of affection and trust you will not think we forget you if we do not send you as frequent tokens of Rememberance as we should do. My wife joins in affectionate rememberance to Mrs. Prince.

I am sincerely your friend
David Buel Jun

In Athens, Prince replied to Judge Buel's letter, telling him of his move there. Other sources report that in Athens Prince devoted himself to the education of his children and enjoyed the cultured atmosphere of the college town, "in the capacity of distinguished advocate and grand gentleman of infinite wit and charm," according to John Wade.

My dear Sir,   *Athens, April 20th 1836*
We have had three separate sittings on your highly welcome letter of the 28th of last month which I received a day or two ago, and it has had its three separate readings of which you may call Mrs. Prince the Senate or <u>upper</u> house, myself the lower and then once in a joint session of both houses and the children. What a triumph is exhibited in your case of the effects of steady persevering firmness & steadiness of purpose. Who could have rationally expected in the year '29–30 the week of which you spent in Georgia, that you would have been able [to] brave such a "Russian Winter" as your last! Steadiness of [purpose] has done much for me, too, but I have never had such trials [as] yours to encounter. My health is more uniform I believe than that of any member of my family; and I wear so slowly that I have been supposed to be my own son. An old gentleman told me last year that although he had not the pleasure of my acquaintance he knew my father very well of the same name who used formerly to attend Oglethorpe Court as a practicing lawyer. Mary's health was better for some weeks after our removal here the first of Feby than it had been for many years and she had gained considerably in flesh; but she was seized with a bleeding of the nose for the first time in her life, that returned so often & held on so obstinately, that before it could be finally stopped had reduced her to her bed and alarmed us all. She had not recovered from that, when taking cold in the only defective tooth she has, the pain she suffered was followed by a swelling of her face that was awful to see. That has at last abated the swelling is subsiding and the fever is leaving her. Oliver re-

mains at the seminary, the Oglethorpe University, lately incorporated by that name in Baldwin County near Milledgeville. His early aversion to his books has been overcome; I cannot say to what precise extent, so far I know, as to present now no serious obstacle to his progress. He is going on in Greek etc creditably & cheerfully. I have favorable accounts of his general deportment & particular studies from sources that I think are candid. Our daughters, Virginia & Frances are with us. Virginia is formed by nature for a scholar; what I most fear, is that she will tend <u>too much</u> to books, she is seldom willingly present without one in her hand. If left entirely to her natural devices she would be a blue-stocking. Frances will be formed more for society & will I think, always be more popular. Mrs. Norman, Mrs. Prince's mother, is still living and has latterly had about her usual unsteady, precarious health. Selina Poe has lately had her third child <u>Mary Prince</u> which was born the night but one before her aunt whose name she bears, left Macon. Mr. Poe has been persuaded to take a Western trip to the Mississippi to purchase lands & will not be back till sometime in June. What has become of Cousin David Hillhouse I know not. I have written to him twice on some little business & can obtain no answer. It is from your letter & that only, I have heard of his intention of going North the ensuing summer; nor have I heard from Mr. Alexander or Mrs. Shepperd's family since December when I saw Mr. A. in Milledgeville.

I have fixed my residence here. I had intended all along to keep hold of the Journal about another year, which was the utmost limit of servitude to which I sentenced myself, but it was impossible. Constitutionally nervous, the duties of that station was so fast wearing that most susceptible part of my system that it would soon have worn it through. Being physically unable longer to continue, I retired a little sooner than I originally intended. I purchased a delightful situation in the county of Habersham under the sunny side of the Blue Ridge. I had stopped here a few days, having got thus far on my removal north but while here some of my friends tempted me with a purchase that I had last year been thinking of, but could not agree with the owners; I say they tempted me again with it, I purchased and here I am, situated not pleasantly this year though I hope to be more so next, for the premises being rented for the year when I purchased, I only, by consent of the tenant, get into one end of the house. We are within a ½ mile of the pleasantest village in Georgia, with schools & churches & good society at hand, fine water, air & health all around. I think & have always thought, that there was no more healthful place in the world. I think it is a little better for my asthmatical disposition than any higher latitude here or at the North would be.

We are planning a visit to the North though not this summer; and if we should go by Charleston we shall before long be able to go quite from here to that place on a railroad which is now in the course of rapid execution to this place. You speak with your usual kindness in your suggestion of our Northern trip & we feel it as we ought. One of the highest pleasures we should experience would be that of seeing you and Cousin Harriet again, and from your gratifying account of your father's health, we have a revering hope of seeing him again. I believe I told you before, that he made a perfect conquest of Mary. I do not know when she has ever been so captivated! Lamenting indeed for they are many who have been removed from us, so that we place a still warmer & tender feeling for those who remain.

We often talk of Mrs. Bellamy, Mrs. Williams & her charming child, of Aunt Hillhouse & every member of her family, of Mr. & Mrs. Schuyler. We have a higher feeling for them than mere gratitude for their abundant kindness to us. Mary loves Mrs. Schuyler like a sister. Pray remember us both to any of them as it may happen in the way. I wonder if Harriet would talk to me with that familiarity that she used to do, when we were like brother and sister now that she has a boy about 16 *months old. No room to speak of the children but give our Love to each & every one of them*

O. H. P.

In Athens, Oliver Hillhouse Prince was revising and enlarging the much admired but slightly out of date *Digest of the Laws of the State of Georgia*. The task was finished in the spring of 1837, and it was now ready for the printer in Boston.

In a letter to his son, Oliver, at school in Lawrenceville, in Gwinnett County, he expressed regret at not being able to visit him before leaving for Boston. Mary added a note containing a very premonitory sentence.

My dear Son   *Athens, May 23d 1837*
I started to Milledgeville last Thursday and got back home on Saturday evening being absent but three days and am now very busy in fixing off for the North. We expect to go to Washington on Thursday & so on to Charleston & thence by Norfolk, Baltimore Phil^a & New York to Boston. I am under promise to be at Boston by the 10th of June but will not be able to reach there as soon, as the Steam Boat in which we go does not leave Charleston till the 2nd and we must be detained a few days in Philadelphia. Your Aunt Sarah Ann is to come up early in the next month and will probably be here when you come down which I understand will be early in July. I suppose Sidney Reese & perhaps Doct. Linton's boys may come down also. Your mother & myself both very much regret that it is not in our power to see you again before we set off. . . . [Bottom part of letter missing] . . . your pleasure, you would find most of that (I mean most pleasure) in the regular & punctual performance of all your duties. I do not know whether you were acquainted with Mr. Sam'l Louthes of Clinton. He died a few days ago of the putrid sore throat I believe. Your mother saw today in a Macon paper that a negro

*woman, Sarah Law, I think they called her, who belonged
to Mr. Goddard of Macon was lately hung at that place, for
having made three attempts to poison her mistress, Mrs.
Goddard.*

*Good bye, my son, for the present. Be a good, a cheerful
& obedient pupil, a pleasant comrade and a dutiful son.
Forever remember, my child, that the greatest portion of
our happiness in this life depends on you. Make our respects to Mr. McAlpin, Mr. Patterson & their families. I
know not without looking over papers, how money matters
stand between me and the school; but however it may be,
all will be squared when I return in the fall. Make my respects to Mr. Martin & to Col. Hutchens when you see
them. Your Grandmother, Mother & sisters all send their
love,*

Your aff' father, Oliver H. Prince

*My own dear Oliver, How can I say that word good bye, it is
a melancholy word to me. I had hoped to go & see you before we left but that has been impossible. My son, if I never
see you more, remember my last words would be "remember your Creator in the days of your youth" for God
has promised "those that seek me early shall find me," read
your Bible & may the spirit of all truth guide you therein is
the constant prayer of your Mother.*

Mary R. Prince

From Boston in June, Prince wrote his last extant letter.
It was addressed to Mary's sister Sarah Ann Wallis and
mother, Mrs. Sarah Norman, the two women who were staying at the Prince's home in Athens with the three children.
Mary added a page telling of her experiences on the trip.

Dear Sarah,   *Boston, June 10th 1837*
*I address this to you in the belief that you will be at Athens
before it arrives. You will have seen my previous letters
from various places, I believe from Augusta, Charleston &*

Philadelphia which will advise you of the several steps of our progress to this latter place. We left Phil[a] day before yesterday (Thursday) at 6 o'clock in the morning in the steam boat "New York", and reached N. York I believe at about 12 or 1 o'clock that day. Then we got into another boat at 5 o'clock P.M., the "Massachusetts," and the next morning (yesterday) arrived at Providence, thence on the Railroad to this place yesterday at 12 or 1. All well, and baggage all safe—which last circumstance I mention in order to caution you if you ever travel by a public conveyance never to take but one parcel, for it seems to me next to a miracle that I saved all ours, three trunks, two bags, a hand box & two umbrellas. Mary is well and, having her with me, I am well also. I know not whether I shall ever travel again after I get home, but certainly never without her. She was much fatigued and worn down in Phil[a], but her spirits and cheerfulness has returned—We had a good nights rest last night, notwithstanding the incipient attempts to fire the town, they tell me there are several attempts every night. Last evening there were three alarms & I suppose as many as five & twenty fire engines each accompanied by a crowd of firemen & other people rushed by the American house where we put up, between an hour by <u>dusk</u> & bed-time, but none afterwards that I know of. I was not at all alarmed by it. You may see by my handwriting that I am nervous, but it is from the excitement of traveling and want of rest. It will take three or four days to restore me. Remember me to all the family & all the servants—I find no letter in the P office

Your afft' brother
<u>*Oliver H. Prince*</u>

My dear Sarah Ann

I do hope you may be at Athens before this reaches there, I feel so much for Mother & the children, they must be lonely. Mrs. Stockton called to see me in Philadelphia and inquired after you, I hardly knew her, she is so re-

duced, I believe the ladies lace tighter than ever & the waists down to the hips, I do not remember to have seen so unbecoming a fashion, the difference in the fashions at the South & North is not so great as formerly, the intercourse is so frequent that we get the style much sooner.

I am not as much pleased as I was with my former visit. I suppose the variety is not so great, Philadelphia is decidedly the handsomest City in the Union; we visited all the principal places, the water works at Fairmount, Girard College, the Mint, the exchange, the Glass works, the big ship, of course though we had been aboard of her before, Mr. Prince would not let me off, I had to stay another day to rest, I could scarcely walk about the room. We went also to see the departure of the Israelites out of Egypt in Diorama, it was the most perfect illusion I ever saw. We should have had a week at least for all we saw. We went ashore at New York and walked around the battery, but it is not to compare with Philadelphia. Boston is a beautiful place, the Mall & Commons is most charming. I have had the house of Mr. Forbes pointed out to me in the Mall, they are considered the Aristocracy & I do not know whether to let them know that I am in the City or not. We heard between Charleston & Norfolk that Cowles had failed, let us know when you write, are we not unfortunate hiring our servants, tell Mrs. Ward we have not seen her friends yet but shall as soon as convenient. I do hope, my dear Sarah, you may all get along with one comfort you have, that we do not, is water, it is ten times as bad as it was when I was here before, it is impossible to wash in it, I do not feel as clean when I am done washing as when I began, soap will not mix with it, how they wash clothes, I can not conceive, I have put out some, I expect they will be awful. You do not know how much I have thought of you, who wash so much. My love to Mother & the children & all friends, do write soon, tell the servants howdy, your ever affectionate sister

Mary R. Prince

In October of 1837, Oliver Hillhouse Prince, his wife, Mary, and servant Frank booked passage for the voyage back to Georgia on the steamship ironically named *Home*. They never reached their destination, for on October 9 the *Home* foundered in the midst of a severe storm and sank off the coast of North Carolina.

Governor George Gilmer in his book *First Settlers of Upper Georgia* told of the tragedy:

About the first of June 1837, my wife and myself left home in company with Mr. and Mrs. Prince, they for Boston and New York, and we for Western Virginia. We four had passed the time of the session of the Legislature of 1824, in the same public house, where we had a private table, and our own drawing-room. Mr. Prince and myself had served in Congress together in 1828–29. We had acted together as trustees of Franklin College, and belonged for many years to the same bar in the practice of the law. Mrs. Prince was a very pretty and exceedingly amiable woman. Mr. Prince was a man of wit and social habits. We went by the way of Charleston to Norfolk.

Mr. Prince went to the north to have printed a new edition of his Digest of the Public Laws of Georgia. When the work was completed, he and Mrs. Prince left New York for their home in the steam vessel, the "Home." The dreadful catastrophe which brought destruction upon that vessel, Mr. and Mrs. Prince, and almost all the passengers, made such an impression upon the whole country, that the event is yet freshly remembered by every one when the bursting of boilers, the burning of steamers, and the wreck of vessels are heard of. Soon after the steamer left New York a violent storm came on, which drove the vessel to the North Carolina coast in a leaking, sinking condition. All were stimulated to do whatever could be done to save the vessel and themselves. Mr. Prince took command of the hands at the pump, where his self-possession and strong strokes showed that he worked for a nobler purpose than fear for his own life. When exhausted by his efforts, he joined his wife to devote himself to her safety. Her self-sacrificing nature would not yield to the temptation of clinging to her husband, when his exertions might be necessary for the safety of all. She urged him to return to his efforts at the pump. Immediately afterwards she attempted to obey the advice of the captain, to remove from one part of the vessel to another less exposed to danger. As she stepped out of the cabin into an open space, a wave passed over and through the vessel, and carried her into the ocean. When the storm subsided, her body was found deposited on the shore. Mr. Prince, resuming his labors at the pump, was spared the pangs of knowing the fate of his wife. To a young man who lived to report the expression, Mr. Prince said, "Remember me to my child, Virginia," what else the uproar of the ocean prevented being heard. No account was ever given of the last struggle for life by those who worked at the pump. In a great heave of the ocean, the vessel parted asunder and went to the bottom.

On October 26, 1837, the *Messenger*, the newspaper in Macon where Oliver and Mary had lived for nine years, reprinted a dramatic eyewitness account which had earlier appeared in a North Carolina newspaper:

Mr. H. Vanderzer, a passenger in the steam packet "Home," passed through this place, this morning, and in a few moments of his stay, gave the particulars of the wreck of that splendid new boat, while on her second trip from N. York to Charleston, and the awful fate of upwards of 60 passengers (among them a large number of ladies) and many of the crew.

His statement corresponds with the following account from the Newbern Spectator of Friday last, received this morning.

On Monday night last, in consequence of stress of weather and the leaky state of the vessel, the captain of the "Home," Captain White, was compelled to bear away for the nearest port.—Either mistaking the entrance at the Bar, or unable to gain it, the boat was driven on shore about six miles north of Ocracock Bar. Our informant, (one of the passengers, who was fortunately rescued from a watery grave) reports, that out of about ninety passengers, and a crew consisting of forty three persons, only twenty of the former, and we know not how many of the latter were saved!

Among the passengers were between thirty and forty ladies, of whom but two escaped. Several children were among those who have been thus hurried to eternity—only one of this class has been saved.

The gale commenced on Sunday afternoon, and the Captain was anxious to double Cape Hatteras, with the intention of anchoring under its lee. About 4 o'clock on Monday, however, the boat commenced leaking so much as to render it necessary for all hands and the passengers to go to the pumps, and to bail, which was continued without intermission until she grounded. The water gained upon them so fast, that at about eight o'clock, the fire was extinguished, and the engine of course was stopped in its operations—a sail was then hoisted, but was immediately blown away. Another was bent, and with this assistance, the boat slowly progressed towards the shore.

At 11 o'clock at night, the "Home" grounded, about 100 yards from the shore. The ladies had all been requested to go forward, as the place where they were more likely to reach the shore, being nearest the beach, but a heavy sea struck her there, and swept nearly one half of them into the sea and they were drowned. One boat was stove at this time. Another small boat was launched, with two or three persons in it, but capsized. The long boat was then put overboard, filled with persons, 25 in number, it is supposed, but did not get 15 feet from the side of the steamer before she upset, and it is the belief of our informant that no one of the individuals in her ever reached the shore. The sea was breaking over the boat at this time with tremendous force, and pieces of her were breaking off at times, floating towards the shore, on some of which persons were clinging. One lady, with a child in her arms, was in the act of mounting the stairs to the upper deck, when the smoke stack fell and doubtless killed her and child on the spot. Some few of the ladies were lashed to the boat—Mrs. Schroeder was confined in this manner to one of the braces of the boat, and another lady was tied to the same piece of timber. Mr. Vanderzer was standing near them, when the latter lady slipped along the brace so that the water broke over her. Mr. V. seized her by the clothes, and held her up for some time, and made every exertion that was possible to release her, but failed. She herself endeavored to unloose the rope, but was unable to do so, and shortly afterwards the brace broke off from the boat, and went towards the shore, Mrs. Schroeder, still fastened to it, while her unfortunate companion, slipped off and was lost. Mrs. S., after striking the beach, with great presence of mind, drew the timber up on the beach so far as to prevent it from being washed away by the waves, and was thus saved.

The hull of the boat broke into three pieces, and the shore was completely strewed with portions of the wreck, baggage, &c. for five or six miles in extent the next morning.

Captain White, with six or seven other persons clung to a piece of the forward part of the boat and reached the beach in safety. Mrs. Lacost floated ashore nearly exhausted, and had she not been taken up would most probably have perished.

Mr. Vanderzer was not the person who was saved by the life preserver, but saved himself by swimming, and was nearly drowned before he reached the land, in encountering a portion of the wreck, of considerable length, which he was obliged to climb over. Mr. H. Anderson was the gen-

tleman who wore the life preserver, and was doubtless entirely indebted to it for his preservation, as he was utterly unable to swim. It was held underneath both his arms, and every sea that struck him, whirled him over once or twice, but he inevitably came "head up," and is, fortunately, a living evidence of the usefulness of this invaluable invention, with which every person who goes to sea should provide themselves.

Mr. Lovegreen was on the upper deck, and tolled the bell of the boat until almost every one had left her, when he sprung off and swam to the land.

We have been thus particular in giving every circumstance, as we know the anxiety that exists, and feel much indebted to Mr. Vanderzer for his kindness in furnishing us with the details.

About 20 of the bodies of the drowned, came ashore before Mr. V. left, and had been interred or preparations were making to perform that melancholy duty for them. . . .

Mr. Vanderzer thinks that there were 22 passengers, and 16 of the crew saved—38 in all. If so, there are two others of the former, whose names are not given.

Most of the passengers remained on the beach all night. Some six or seven, however found their way to the light house, several miles off; among them two or three of the crew, entirely divested of their clothing.

Messrs. Vanderzer, Bishop, Anderson and Holmes, got on board a brig, and came to Newbern; and it is probable that the remainder will take the same route, as there are vessels leaving almost daily. One boy took passage in a vessel bound to the North.

The boat had entirely disappeared, all her wood work having floated off, and her machinery imbedded in the sand.

Thus we close the account of the loss of the ill fated "Home," sympathizing with the mourning relatives and friends of those who found a watery grave, and participating in the joyful feelings of such as have been rescued from *destruction.—Long may it be before it becomes our duty to record another such a calamitous and heart rending disaster. . . .*

On Thursday, October 26, 1837, the *Messenger* printed the obituary of the Princes.

> *"Friend after friend departs:*
> *Who hath not lost a friend?*
> *There is no union here of hearts,*
> *That finds not here an end."*

Perished, by the wreck of the steam packet "Home," on her voyage from New York to Charleston, on the night of the 9th inst. OLIVER H. PRINCE, ESQ. and his wife, MARY R. PRINCE, the former a native of Connecticut, who came to this State in early youth, and the latter of Georgia.

Mr. Prince left Athens (the place of his residence,) in May last, for Boston, to superintend the printing of a Digest of the Laws of Georgia, which he had recently compiled by authority of the Legislature; and having completed his work, embarked, in company with his wife, on board the above packet, fondly hoping very soon to meet their children, whom they had left behind. But Heaven had otherwise ordered; and in obedience to that decree, they both perished in the same wave. . . .

Mr. Prince for more than twenty-five years was a practitioner of Law in this State, and though not an eloquent speaker, was at all times interesting and convincing. Truth was his polar star, and to arrive at that, he regarded not the ruggedness of the way. He was well versed in the hidden mysteries of this intricate science and avoided no labor in the preparation of causes involving doubtful legal principles. He was safe in counsel, and scrupulously honest in all matters of trust and confidence. As a writer, he was spirited, perspicuous and witty. . . .

Mrs. Prince had been for more than ten years a consis-
tent member of the Presbyterian Church, and her conduct
in life was regulated by christian principle. They have both
left a large circle of friends and devoted relatives to mourn
their untimely end. The chasm thus made in the family
circle can never be supplied, for they were the life and
spirit of the whole—the centre around which the other
members revolved. This sad bereavement, so unusual in its
circumstances, addresses a voice of warning to all—"Be ye
also ready, for at an hour ye think not, the Son of man
cometh."

NOTES TO PART I

1. James Hillhouse once reminisced that his father "in the days
of steady habits, came up on his Narraganset pacer and took his
seat in one hundred and six legislatures [then semiannual], was a
tall spare man, as dark as the Black Douglas himself, and did not
particularly fancy being hit upon his reputed Mohegan cross.

"Being the Patriarch of the eastern section of the state, and
with a relish of wit, he usually had a circle round him at his
lodgings.

"On a certain occasion, I, who had often, in the State Legislature been opposed in argument to him, but was then a young
member of Congress, happened to call upon him during the
Hartford session, at a moment when he was reading with great
glee to his friends, a squib upon the Congressmen from a Philadelphia newspaper. It was at the time a Library was talked of for
Congress. The gist of the pleasantry lay in the adaption of a book
to the private history of each of the prominent members. The old
man read on, chuckling, for some time, at last, looking up, he
said, dryly, 'Why Jemmy, they don't notice you at all'—'Read on,
father.' He did so and soon came to the volume to be ordered for
his son, namely, 'A History of the Aborigines' to aid him in tracing
his pedigree! For a rarity, the old gentleman was floored.

"Well do I remember those stupendous shoe-buckles, that
long gold-headed cane, (kept in Madam, thy Sister's best closet
for thy sole annual use), that steel watch-chain and silver pen-
dants, yea, and the streak of holland, like the slash in an antique
doublet, commonly seen betwixt thy waist-coat and small clothes,
as thou passedst daily, at nine o'clock, A.M., during the autumnal session.

"One of his little grand-daughters took it into her head to watch for her dear 'Black Grandpapa,' and insist on kissing him in the street, as he passed. He condescended, once or twice, to stoop for her salute; but, anon, we missed him. He passed us no more; having adopted Church street, instead of Temple street on his way to the Council Chamber.

"One of the earliest recollections of our boyhood, is the appearance of that Council Chamber, as we used to peep into it. Trumbull sat facing the door—clarum et venerabile nomen!—there lay his awful sword and cocked hat,—and round the table, besides his Excellency and his Honor, were twelve noble-looking men, whom our juvenile eyes regarded as scarcely inferior to gods.

"As the oldest Counsellor, at the Governor's right hand, sat, ever, the Patriarch of Montville (a study for Spagnoletto,) with half his body, in addition to his legs, under the table, a huge pair of depending eyebrows concealing all the eyes he had, till called upon for an opinion, when he lifted them up long enough to speak briefly, then they immediately relapsed.

"He resigned his seat, at the age of eighty in full possession of his mental power.

"The language of the letter before me is; 'He has withdrawn from public life with cheerfulness and dignity' He was able, at that age, to ride his Narraganset from New Haven to New London in a day, abhorring 'wheel carriages'. At his leave-taking, I have been told, there was not a dry eye at the Council Board."

2. The Connecticut School Fund's property was scattered throughout five states, some parts of which were difficult to reach.

James Hillhouse later recalled: "The toils I under-went were curious and interesting. I was in journeyings often, in watchings often, in hunger and thirst, in perils from robbers, in perils from the wilderness.

"Once I was frost-bitten, losing in consequence,—during the greater part of one winter and far from my family—, the use of one eye.

"I was arrested as a criminal by an enraged debtor, who in his own neighborhood exercised a party influence, and barely escaped the indignity of prison.

"Twice I almost died of fevers caused by the unsettled and unwholesome regions I was obliged to visit.

"On one occasion, while riding on horseback in the wilderness for seventy miles, I pushed my horse, Jinny, for thirty miles more without stopping, as two ruffians were following me. I escaped with twenty thousand dollars of public money.

"On one of my school fund journeys, traversing a forest in Ohio, which, for many a long mile had seemed as undisturbed by human occupants as on the day of creation, there suddenly glided into the path an armed Indian. The apparition was rather startling. The Sachem nodded, however, to his compatriot, and kept jogging on, as if unconcerned. The Indian surveyed me earnestly, from time to time; but, whether young Jin quickened or slackened her pace, he still kept at the wheel. After about six miles, the sulky drew up, and a four pence ha' penny was handed to its persevering attendant. The Redskin received it with a grunt, or nod of thanks, turned off into the woods, and was seen no more.

"If any evil purpose was harboured, perhaps the donor owed something, on this occasion, to those indisputable sachem marks, which distinguish both my person and aspect."

Part II

Washington Poe, circa 1840.
Attributed to John Beale Bordley by the
Frick Art Reference Library.
Photograph by Ken Hill.

Washington Poe

When the news reached Georgia of the disastrous sinking of the *Home*, with such a toll of lives, it was said that shock waves reverberated throughout the state. Such accidents at sea were not uncommon. Prince himself, in his newspaper, had noted with great sadness that a young neighbor drowned in just such a tragedy, though the number of lives lost was not nearly so large.

In the untimely death of Prince, Georgia had lost a man who was extremely popular and prominent in many of the state's affairs. His name had been foremost in many educational, industrial, and political matters. He was known and admired not only in the capital of Milledgeville, but throughout the state. It was a profound tragedy; the loss had indeed left a deep chasm among the friends of the Princes, but more especially in the close family left behind. The loss would never be filled or completely forgotten.

To the brother-in-law of Oliver Hillhouse Prince fell the task of picking up the pieces of the shattered lives of the three orphaned children. In 1837, the year of Prince's death, no one had been more active and influential in the growth and prosperity of Macon than Washington Poe. The population of the town had increased greatly, and with this growth came the need for churches, schools, banks, and other public institutions. In the organization of these establishments he gave fully of his time, talents, and money. In later years it would be written of him that a history of his life and his experiences would be a history of Macon. Upon Poe's death in 1876, the Macon bar passed the following resolution:

There is no person among the living or dead, who has been so long and so prominently identified with the history of our city. When he settled here, Macon was a small village. The courthouse was a rough, wooden building on Mulberry Street. The county jail was a structure of logs which occupied the site of Christ Church. Fifth Street was the fashionable residential section of the town. He saw the organization of the corporation, the laying of the corner-stone of its churches, colleges, and public institutions, the breaking of ground for its railroads, and was its Mayor, its alderman, and its attorney.

Washington Poe was born in Augusta, Georgia, on July 13, 1800, into a family whose history and connections were as varied as those of Oliver Prince's family. His father, William Poe, born in 1755 in Lancaster County, Pennsylvania, migrated to Georgia in 1789 to claim a land grant he received as a result of service as a sergeant in the Revolutionary War. William's brother, David Poe, born in Ireland in 1743, was a versatile man who moved to Baltimore sometime prior to the outbreak of the American Revolution. Records show that his occupations ranged from furniture-maker and wheelwright to that of a soldier who helped drive the British and Tories out of Baltimore. In 1778, he was appointed Assistant Deputy Quartermaster of the Continental Army with the rank of major. He was said to have been of great assistance to General Lafayette, who during his journey to America in 1824–25, visited the grave of David Poe and exclaimed, "Ici repose un coeur noble" (here rests a noble heart).

"General" Poe, as he was known, not only fought with valor for his country, but contributed $40,000 to the cause, which was never repaid. His wife, Elizabeth Cairnes, also shared in his energy and patriotism. During the Revolutionary War, when Lafayette was in Baltimore, she cut with her own hands five hundred pieces of clothing for his ragged troops, and superintended the sewing of them for the soldiers.

In 1814, at the age of seventy-one, David Poe again volunteered and saw active fighting against the British in the Battle of North Point.

David Poe's son, David Jr., became in 1809 the father of the famed writer Edgar Allan Poe, who during the 1840's corresponded with his relative Washington Poe in Macon.[1]

My Dear Sir,   *Philadelphia, August 15th (1840)*
On the other leaf of this sheet you will find the Prospectus of a Magazine which I am about attempting to establish, and of which the first number will be issued on the first of January next. When I was editor of the Southern Messenger you were so kind as to use your influence in behalf of that Journal, although I had myself no proprietary right in it and derived only a collateral benefit from your exertions. May I ask you to assist me in the present instance? Your brothers in Augusta have kindly offered me every aid in their power, and I have reason to hope that you will also feel inclined to do so for the sake of the relationship which exists between us, and for the honor of our family name. Upon looking over my Prospectus I trust you will find my purposes, as expressed in it, of a character worthy of your support. I am activated by an ambition which I believe to be an honourable one—the ambition of serving the great cause of truth; while endeavouring to forward the literature of the country. You are aware that hitherto my circumstances, as regards pecuniary matters, have been bad. In fact, my path in life has been beset with difficulties from which I hope to emerge by this effort. So far, my exertions have served only to enhance my literary reputation in some degree and to benefit others *so far as money was concerned. If I succeed in the present attempt, however, fortune & fame must go hand in hand—and for these reasons I now most earnestly solicit your support. My chances of*

establishing the Magazine depend upon my getting a certain number of subscribers previously to the first of December. This is rendered necessary by my having no other capital to begin with than whatever reputation I may have acquired as a literary man. Had I money, I might issue the first numbers without this list, but as it is, at least 500 names will be required to enable me to commence. I have no doubt in the world that this number can be obtained among those friends who aided me in the Messenger, but still it behooves me to use every exertion to ensure success. I think it very probable that your influence in Macon will procure for me several subscribers, and, if so, you will render me a service for which I shall always be grateful. Remember me kindly to your family, and believe me

Yours most truly
Edgar A. Poe

Knowledge of the ancestry of Poe's mother, Frances Winslow, is slight. Aside from the family tradition that she was a descendant of Edward Winslow, little else is known but that her marriage to William Poe took place in Augusta on March 5, 1795. In the short span of seven years, Frances Winslow Poe gave birth to four children, William Jr., Washington, Robert, and Matilda Ann. On July 22, 1802, Frances died, to be followed in death by William on September 13, 1804.

The four young children became the wards of Thomas Cumming, a close friend of the Poes. Cumming, an influential banker and the first mayor of Augusta, reared and educated the Poe children with great fidelity. In 1818 Matilda Ann Poe became the wife of her guardian's son, Joseph Cumming.

Apparently William Poe did not leave his children penniless, since records show many legal transactions of land and cash to them. Washington, second son of his father, in his early years was educated at the Sand Hill Academy in

Augusta, and sent later to a school in New Jersey to pre-pare for admission to Princeton. When ready to enter col-lege, he became impatient and returned to Augusta to en-ter into the warehouse and commission business with his brothers, Robert and William. Becoming dissatisfied, he again returned north and enrolled in the celebrated law school of Judge Gould at Litchfield, Connecticut, where he remained during the year of 1824.

It was not all work and no play for the aspiring young lawyer in Litchfield, however, for many years later he re-cited from memory some humorous poems he composed during his stay there.

Litchfield, Conn., March 1824
The circumstances under which the following lines were written are these. Several gentlemen of Litchfield were in the habit of visiting certain young ladies on Wednesday evenings for conversation. Each one by turns contributed original pieces among which Terry, Mansfield and myself were members. Terry was a large good looking man rather fond of wine. Mansfield was a great student, but unfortu-nately fell in love. Holmes was a young Doctor. The last night we met, I for Cambridge left the following Will to be read at the next meeting.

W. Poe Sr.

A WILL
In Principis, I give to the great Mr. Terry
Six bottles once filled with the best of old cherry
The bottles are empty and cherry there's none
They have the rich fragrance, the cherry's done
In Litchfield, there's none to be had very fine
Their fashion is plain, but that won't be known
If with best of old stuff, they are always shown.
To Lord Mansfield, the best of all our good fellows,
In Secundo I give a pair of old bellows

Some hundreds of stanzas of rhymes not the best,
To serve as a solace for lovers distressed.
A Lamp of Japan well replenished with oil,
To illume his path when at midnight he'll toil.
A pair of old snuffers its light to renew,
An extinguisher useful when labor is through.
In Tertis I give to Holmes—not a quack,
Six pills and a Dose of the famed Ipecac.
A Knife that has given me many a bleeding,
A Treatise on Farriery good for his reading.
One vial I'll add to end my bequest,
Of Laudanum most famous for putting to rest.
Twenty drops is a dose for all new beginners,
But sixty won't do for the most hardened sinners
Now lastly I ask oh! could these be given,
A Treasure to mortal directly from Heaven,
That alone would be worthy on those to bestow
Who deserve richer gifts then we meet with below.
But vain the request—though sincere it arise,
And plainly it's fragrance assends to the skies.
Then all I can offer is friendship sincere
And that like their virture shall bloom all the year.
Thus ends my bequest to all my good friends
And if it be faulty can make no amends.
So wishing them all a happy old age
I bid them farewell and push off the stage.

Litchfield
1824

I was invited to spend an evening with some young ladies. I declined going, but sent them the following couplet.

I'd rather silent sit all day
Than talk and talk and nothing say,
Or mark the weather foul or fair,
Of which all know or nothing care

*To this the ladies replied in a most severe manner. I then
wrote the following lines by way of apology.*

> *Oh! Spare me courteous Ladies, spare,*
> *I cannot female censure bear.*
> *To be the cause of your distain,*
> *Doth work like madness in my brain.*
> *Reproach from those we scarcely know*
> *Doth give the heart full many a throw*

Washington Poe returned to Georgia after completion of
his law course and was admitted to the bar in May of 1825.
In that same month he came to Macon, his home for the
next fifty-one years, at a time when, in the words of John
Butler, "The ring of the axe echoed through the new village, as the settlers built their homes."

A contemporary described the new young lawyer as
"erect, tall, stately and impressive, his figure slender, with a
gracefulness of manner, filling the full measure of the term
'a perfect gentleman.' So deep was the impression that
none dared to dub him colonel or judge. He was simply
Mr. Poe. Standing alone in this respect, the genteel but
worn-out old title of Mister became with him a distinction.
I fancy from his general demeanor and his history he was
of the opinion, that to be a true and refined gentleman,
and so recognized by everyone, was a greater title than any
official title."

After entering into law practice with Oliver Prince, Washington Poe was elected Intendent of the new town and took
office in January 1827, succeeding Edward Dorr Tracy.

On December 24, 1829, he and Selina Shirley Norman,
Mary Prince's sister, were married. Selina, though only
fourteen, was a self-possessed young woman whose civic
spirit and resolution were to culminate many years later
when Macon citizens faced the anxiety and excitement of
the Civil War. In 1861 she organized the Ladies' Soldiers'

Relief Society and served for four years as its president. Under her direction, thousands of garments were made and sent to the soldiers; hospital supplies were collected and placed at the disposal of the surgeon general, Dr. James Mercer Green, and the hospital quartermaster, Major G. R. Fairbanks; money was raised by her zeal and untiring efforts, and $7,391.85 was made available to the society during the first seven months of its existence.

When Macon became the headquarters for state hospitals, groups of women went daily to minister to the wants and needs of the hospitalized sick and dying soldiers. During the last year of the war there were 6,000 disabled soldiers in Macon who were cared for by the Ladies' Soldiers' Relief Society.

Every train bringing soldiers to the hospitals, and every train passing through Macon bearing sick and wounded troops, was met by committees from the relief society, who distributed food and clothing where needed. Conveyances were provided for carrying the soldiers to the hospitals. In 1862 the old Macon Hotel, where Lafayette was entertained in 1825, was given to the relief society and was converted into a hospital and "Wayside Inn" where soldiers passing through Macon, returning to and from the battlefields, were housed and fed, and where the sick were cared for.

All this work from 1861 until the close of the war in 1865 was under the direct supervision and management of Mrs. Poe, whose faithful adherence to duty throughout the four years of the war proved a stimulus to those who worked with her.

In 1831, when Macon was still a rough frontier town, much lawlessness occurred. Poe, who by this time was Solicitor-General of the circuit, often accompanied the intimidated sheriff to the armed lodgings of the offender to assist in making the arrest, though carrying no weapon himself.

In 1840, when he was again mayor, election riots broke out in the town. A party of excited men broke through the windows of the courthouse, overpowered the managers, and destroyed the ballot box. Washington Poe went at once to the scene and, speaking to the agitated men, urged them to dispel all excitement and aid him in the performance of his municipal authority. By his prompt and determined action he subdued the disturbance, and without use of a weapon brought every disturber of the peace to jail to await his trial before the proper court. "The brandishments of weapons and the threats of assassination had no effect upon the Mayor," reported John Butler.

As a lawyer, Washington Poe was known for his constant attention to all the details of office practice, while in the courtroom he was effective, thorough, eloquent, and persuasive. His success as a lawyer was due in part to his high sense of personal and professional honor. Although he neither sought nor desired political office, he once yielded to the pleas of his numerous friends and allowed his name to be placed in nomination as a Whig candidate for Congress. He was overwhelmingly elected, but resigned before taking office under a sense of duty to his family and his many clients. (His large practice extended throughout the state.)

A religious man, he became a member of the Presbyterian church in November 1828, and the following year was made a ruling elder.

When the Princes went down on the *Home*, the tremendous duty of administering their estate, caring for the three children, and comforting the other members of the bereaved family fell to Washington Poe and would demand much of his time and attention during the next nine years.

Since Oliver Prince had died intestate, his large estate must have caused Poe an immense problem.[2] The real estate included homes and acreage in Macon, Milledgeville, and Athens. There were large assets of cash, railroad stocks, and other properties. The inventory, completed in December 1837, listed in great detail perishable property of books, furniture, household goods, notes of due bills, and slaves.[3]

An estimate of the value of Prince's estate could be made by the large bond of $50,000 required for its administration. The sale of his possessions was held at Athens in March of 1838, with R. Rogers as auctioneer. The books in Prince's library, offered first in the auction, showed his wide interests. They ranged from history, law, philosophy, chemistry, travels, geography, engineering, economy, and rhetoric, to bound volumes of Blackwood, *North American Review*, *Spectator*, and the *Southern Review*. There were also sixty bound volumes of documents on the United States Senate and House of Representatives, and the state of Georgia.

The inventory listed one amazing title, *Westward Ho!*, appearing over twenty years before its more famous Kingsley namesake. This book, however, was written by James K. Paulding, a literary associate of Washington Irving, and had been reviewed in the *Georgia Journal*. Although the review was not written by Prince (it was credited to the *Southern Literary Messenger*), the book interested him and had been added to his own library.

Seven volumes of Shakespeare purchased by Oliver Prince in 1813 for $4.62½ were duly listed in the inventory. Though then noted "complete," when sold to an Athens buyer they were called a "broken set." As three of the volumes are extant, a fascinating but pathetic little story can be assumed to be true. A little girl tiptoed into her father's library the night before the sale and removed the three miniature books. It was perhaps all that Virginia thought she had left of her adored father's possessions.

The appraised prices and the amounts realized for the treasure trove of books in Prince's library would make today's bibliophile weep bitter tears. No book was priced higher than $20.00, this for the sixty volumes of government documents. The prices then descended from $12.00 for a twelve-volume bound set of *North American Review*, $6.00 for four volumes of leather-bound books, *Jefferson's Works*, $3.00 for a three-volume set of *British Lives*, to a price of $1.00 for four volumes of Mitford's *Our Village*. This last was almost certainly an American first edition (1824–32).

The books, nevertheless, did not realize their estimated value. *British Lives* brought $1.50, *Jefferson's Works* $4.00, *North American Review* $9.00 (bought by Washington Poe) and the four volumes of *Our Village*, the small sum of $.80. William Norman, Prince's brother-in-law, purchased four bound volumes of the *Georgia Journal* for $8.00 and the sixty-volume set of government documents remained unsold.

The beautiful furniture, some of it chosen so carefully by the Princes on their northern trip, was eagerly acquired by the residents of Athens who attended the auction. From the elegant furnishings of the parlor, through the bedrooms' feather beds, hair mattresses, wardrobes, dressing glasses, bureaus and chests, the dining room's mahogany tables and wine stands, to the outbuildings and their content, all were sold to the highest bidder.

A small barouche and a larger one sold for $220 and $240, respectively, while a chest of tools brought $50.00. One thousand seven hundred and fifty feet of lumber realized $24.79, and a short-tail cow and yearling yielded $10.00. And so on; the list was long, even Oliver Jr.'s pony was sold to A. B. Daniels for $31.25.

Although the three Prince children may not have been present at the auction, the sensitive Virginia undoubtedly was aware of it. The memory of the traumatic days when she first learned of her parents' tragic deaths never left her, for although she lived to be quite old, her granddaughter recalled that she never spoke of her father without tears filling her eyes.

The extensive sale of Oliver Prince's property did not include some items. Three oil portraits, listed in the inventory, did not appear in the sales list. These, along with a few small purchases in the children's name, were brought back to Macon. The last entry on the sale record showed a purchase of a wagon and two horses, bought by Washington Poe for $300. His meticulous records noted also that in March 1838, Balaam, one of Prince's servants, made two separate trips to Athens to bring back other belongings. Balaam, a trusted and reliable man, made the journeys alone, and later, in 1841, worked for the city council in Macon.

Although Washington Poe assumed the care of the three Prince children, it was not until November of 1841 that he was legally appointed the guardian of Virginia and Frances, as by then Oliver Jr. was eighteen. From the time of the death in 1837 of his brother-in-law until the two girls married, Poe had the sole responsibility for their care and education.

In addition to administering Prince's large estate, Poe had the difficult task of maintaining sixteen Negro servants. None were ever sold, although through the years several were lent to relatives for support. One, named George, was apprenticed to a Mr. Sledge to learn the trade of blacksmithing, but all remained Poe's responsibility until they were divided among the Prince children in 1844. By then, however, one of the charges was gone. Poe, in the estate records, wrote in a barely discernible script "Fr. lost." Frank, Oliver Prince's favorite servant, had been with his master throughout the almost four years in Milledgeville and had accompanied the Princes on their fateful trip to Boston. He also went down on the *Home*.

Indicative of the affection this southern family felt for

their servants, Dr. Green, Virginia's husband, wrote in the family Bible in October 1863, "Susan, a beloved & faithful servant died of typhoid fever in Roswell (Edward's nurse)."

One of the major problems Poe had with the Prince estate was the home in Milledgeville. Listed in his estate records as the "Rockwell Mansion," the home has been pictured and described in many architectural books published throughout the years. It has been the subject of many newspaper articles, and has recently been placed on the National Register of Historic Buildings.

Although the date of the house's construction varied with each printing—sometimes stated as 1834, other times given as 1837—its architect and builder was invariably named as Joseph Lane, a carpenter and housewright of Milledgeville. An examination of conflicting dates, however, shows that the facts must be otherwise. Dismissing the construction date of 1837, which would have made it impossible for Prince to have owned it as his death occurred in that year, plus the fact that he had moved away from Milledgeville in *1835*, the remaining date of 1834 made the probability of Joseph Lane as its builder impossible, as records show that he did not arrive in Milledgeville until the fall of 1837. There are no existing records of the house's construction.

Prince's letters, journals, and his estate records reveal the fact that *he* must have been the builder of the Rockwell Mansion, possibly between 1832 and 1835. His 1832 Milledgeville expense book stopped abruptly in August of that year, leaving a few blank pages as if he had decided there was no room for listing extensive expenditures and adopted another book. There were other significant entries. In April 1832 he paid a fifty-cent fee for "Stetwell," and in July 1833 a notation read "½ of grant fee $5.00." Also, there were many large purchases of beef and bacon as if he may have been buying provisions for some of his servants, who may very possibly have been building the house. Frank's presence in Milledgeville was very definitely established by the numerous notations of "shoes and clothing for Frank," and a single notation of "Frank's board" on March 22, 1832. There was also a significant increase in Prince's taxes between 1832 and 1833.

In his letter of July 15, 1834, to his cousin Judge Buel of Troy, New York, Prince asked Buel to deliver an enclosed letter to Ayers and Thayer concerning the construction of twenty blinds (the exact number of windows in the Rockwell house), and "venture to name you as my Banker again," pointing to the possibility that he had obtained other building material from the same source.

In the letter from J. H. Lloyd to Prince (June 18, 1835), Lloyd asked for the return of his portfolio of architectural drawings, which he had lent him and which Prince had had in his possession for quite some time, indicating that he was apparently referring to the design book while building the house.

Although Oliver Prince, in the Rockwell Mansion's history, is listed as the second of its seven prominent Milledgeville resident-owners, it is almost a certainty that he never lived in it, as his letter of April 13, 1835, again to Judge Buel, states, "We still board at a boarding house, but shall resume housekeeping after next year."

In the fall of 1835, Prince left Milledgeville for Athens, selling the *Georgia Journal* to William S. Rockwell, and apparently the perhaps unfinished house to Samuel Rockwell, William's father. Hence its name "Rockwell," as the Rockwells were the first to live in it.

The curious circumstances that caused the house to return to Prince's ownership (this time to his estate) are revealed in the entries Washington Poe made in the detailed administration records he kept.

Apparently, William Rockwell was sued for the money owed Prince, for on May 21, 1838, Poe wrote in the records

as a credit, "William S. Rockwell on <u>Judgement</u> $1100.00."
Samuel Rockwell was also involved as on January 9, 1839, a
notation read, "S. Rockwell $1966.00," and again on April
26 of the same year, "S. Rockwell in part $500.00." Samuel
Rockwell died on August 4, 1841. On May 1, 1842, Poe
noted as a credit, "To cash from William & Samuel Rockwell & Thomas Butler King on notes contained in the appraisement $7,144.73."

Thomas Butler King, a prominent Georgia lawyer, had
evidently been engaged by the Rockwells to try to rescue
them from their financial difficulties with the Prince estate.
Evidently he succeeded, because in November of the same
year Poe wrote in the records, "Deduct amount Rockwells
& King's notes, they being changed in the appraisement
$7,144.73."

During this period when property was sold the seller
gave a bond or note to the purchaser stating that when the
full amount of the purchase had been paid the deed would
be given to the purchaser. Since Samuel Rockwell had never
paid the full amount—Poe collected only about $3500
from the Rockwells, probably the amount agreed upon for
the newspaper—the note became invalid. After a period of
six years, in which Poe waited patiently for the money to be
paid the estate for the house, he finally repossessed it. On
July 5, 1843, he noted in the records, "Expenses to Milledgeville to make title to house $6.50." Thus the Rockwell
Mansion reverted again to the Prince estate.

One of the many legends told of the house was that every
one of its marble mantels was cracked, the damage done by
an axe or hammer, supposedly by Mrs. Rockwell. It was reported that she felt if she could not enjoy the house, neither would anyone else. Apropos of this, Washington Poe
bought an insurance policy for the house on May 1, 1841.

Most likely the Rockwell house was not completely
finished, since on January 1, 1842, Poe's record notes,
"Cash paid John S. Stephens for work on Rockwell house

$2600.00." This notation explains the variable interior of
the house. The rooms on the left side were finished in an
elegant style derived from an Asher Benjamin design book
published in Boston in 1833, while the woodwork in the
opposite rooms was much simpler and varied from room to
room, as if it had been a local carpenter's handiwork.

The history of the house did not end at this point, as
there were several notations of rent collected for it even
after Poe wrote in the records on September 1, 1843, "H. V.
Johnson, 2 notes for purchase of Rockwell Mansion, viz 1st
due 1st January 1844, $1250.00 1 due 1st January 1845
with interest from 1st January, 1844 for $1250.00."

Governor Herschel V. Johnson must have eventually
paid for the house, because in August of 1854 he sold it.
The indenture read in part, "eight acres . . . being known
as the Rockwell place conveyed to said Herschel V. Johnson
by Washington Poe as the administrator of Oliver H. Prince,
deceased, and Thomas Ragland." Thomas Ragland, Prince's
partner in the *Georgia Journal*, had also sold his interest in
the newspaper to William Rockwell. The appearance of his
name on the indenture as co-owner of the Rockwell house
makes it seem likely that the house and newspaper were
sold together.

Samuel Rockwell's estate was never finally settled until
1861, and at that time his debts were described in the legal
records as, "each of said bills, claiming by different right,
large sums of money, more than was in possession of the
administrator or derivable from the estate."

Over the years, the old Rockwell Mansion has withstood
vandalism, fire, and the ravages of time. One owner sold
the beautiful Asher Benjamin-inspired woodwork from the
dining room to the Winterthur Museum, Wilmington, Delaware, to be restored and displayed there in the museum's
"Georgia Room." Winterthur research experts stated that
the woodwork may have been made in New England. To-

day the house stands proud and beautiful in the Midway community of Milledgeville.

Even while extricating the many problems of the Prince estate, Washington Poe was centrally involved in the civic life of his city and state. In 1840, while serving as mayor, he was a delegate from Bibb County and speaker at the convention held in Macon to ratify the anti-Van Buren slate (William Harrison for President, John Tyler for Vice President) nominated earlier in Milledgeville. An admirer of Henry Clay, Poe was elected president of the Clay Club in 1844, the year in which he was elected to the United States House of Representatives.

In November 1849 Poe was speaker at a mass meeting in Macon called for the citizens to express opposition to the state legislature's railroad policies. At the meeting he was also selected to serve on the commission assigned to draft a protest to legislation interfering with a railroad connection at Macon. (Earlier he had been a delegate to the 1836 General Railroad Convention in Knoxville, Tennessee.)

Addressing the Union party's meeting in Macon on September 28, 1850, he submitted a set of resolutions supporting recent acts of Congress regarding the admission of new states. In the heated November elections, he was chosen as a Union delegate to the Milledgeville convention called by Governor Towns to consider Georgia's response to the congressional legislation. By a vote of 237 to 19, the convention resolved that Georgia should resist a disruption of the Union by any act of Congress "incompatible with the safety, domestic tranquility, the rights and honor of the Slaveholding States."

Presiding over a meeting called in Macon on the day of the 1860 national election, Poe cautioned the citizenry to be calm and deliberate in their response to the election of Abraham Lincoln. In January he was one of the three Bibb

County delegates to the Milledgeville convention at which Georgia seceded from the Union. When war came, he was detailed to the post office in Macon.

In the years after the war he continued to participate in public life. In 1870 he delivered the main address at the cornerstone laying ceremony for the new Bibb County courthouse at the corner of Mulberry and Second streets in Macon. Two years later he served as a Bibb County delegate to the September state-wide Democratic convention.

Washington Poe died on October 1, 1876. On October 3 the *Macon Telegraph* advised its readers of the city's loss:

We are pained to announce the death of the Nestor of [the] Macon Bar, Hon. Washington Poe. He expired at his residence in this city Sunday night while the public clocks were striking the hour of twelve. He had lived to a ripe and honorable old age—having passed the 76th anniversary of his birth. . . . Apparently of slender and delicate frame, such, however, was the elasticity and vigor of his constitution that, but for untoward events in the last ten or twelve years, he would probably have lasted much longer. The anxieties and losses of the war impoverished him—impaired his ability to sustain the demands of his professional business, at a time when its gains were most needed; and last week the death of a loved son in the flower of manhood was a shock from which he never rallied. Mr. Poe was prostrate on his bed when the corpse of his son was carried from the house, and gradually sank thenceforward to the response of death.

He was buried in Rose Hill Cemetery.

Sarah Virginia Prince—
James Mercer Green

The young doctor to whom Virginia Prince was married on May 5, 1846, had established his practice in Macon in the same unhappy year of 1837 that she had come to live with her Aunt Selina and Uncle Washington Poe. But it was not in this city that the two had first become acquainted. While Virginia's father, Oliver Prince, published the *Georgia Journal* in Milledgeville, James Mercer Green was also a resident of the capital. In 1817 his father, William Montgomery Green, had come to the town from Athens to establish two private academies.

The elder Green, a tall dignified gentleman who always carried a red bandanna silk handkerchief and took snuff from a gold snuff box, had led a fascinating life. Born in Ireland in 1767 of a family prominent in political circles, he had been educated at Trinity College in Dublin. His first wife, Anna Maria Wilkes, was a niece of John Wilkes, the lord mayor of London, famous for his sympathy with the American cause during the Revolution.

Green, an ardent patriot of Ireland, had once been offered a seat in the English Parliament but had refused the honor, stating that he would accept no favors from a government who oppressed his countrymen. He had been extremely active in the Irish rebellion of 1798, and was arrested and imprisoned in Newgate Prison, Dublin, and later removed to Fort George, Scotland, where he was released on condition that he leave the Empire. Spending the winter of 1802–1803 in Brussels, and that of 1803–1804 in

Sarah Virginia Prince Green.
Artist unknown.
A May 5, 1841, entry in Washington Poe's records of the
Oliver Hillhouse Prince estate lists "Portrait Va. &
Frame $69.00."
Photograph by J. Carol Gore.

James Mercer Green,
circa 1845. Artist unknown.
Photograph by Ken Hill.

Paris, he, in company with Thomas Addis Emmet, brother of the unfortunate Irish hero Robert Emmet, sailed on October 4, 1804, from Bordeaux, France, for America.

The descendants long believed that this progenitor of the family in America adopted the name Green as a symbol of his beloved Emerald Isle. He always wore on his little finger a delicate ring in which the name Nugent was engraved. There were also silver spoons engraved with the same lettering, which the family of his first wife inherited. Green's last words were the whispered name "Nugent," repeated over and over.

Arriving in New York on November 11, 1804, Green found the climate of the North too severe for his wife's failing health, and migrated south, first to Beaufort, South Carolina, then to Savannah, and finally to Athens, Georgia. Several years later, after the death of his first wife in 1807, Green married Jane McKonkey of Burke County near Louisville, Georgia. James Mercer Green was born on November 15, 1815, in Athens, where his father was a professor of mathematics and languages at Franklin College. Shortly afterward, William Green moved to Milledgeville. There in the capital his two private academies (one of which was for young women) had an advanced and comprehensive curriculum, but the tuition was costly and probably restricted the number of students enrolled.

While he struggled to establish his schools in Milledgeville, Jane McKonkey Green and her children lived in her relatives' home in Louisville. Three of her extant letters were addressed to her husband in Milledgeville, while the remaining three were sent to him in care of the courthouse in Telfair County, where he may have gone in search of more students for the schools. (The often-mentioned Thomas was Green's fifteen-year-old son by his first wife, Anna Maria. Kollock and Ann are his two other children by Jane.)

Louisville

My Dear Husband,   *March 9th 1819*

I merely write to let you hear that I am still on my feet and rather better than when you left. When Thomas comes I will thank you to send me in addition to the things I told T. of, to bring a pair of those thin linnen sheets in my trunk. David is commenced a frolick today, James had a return of fever on Sunday & Koll is much better and chatters like a parrot. I should be really comfortable in my present circumstances, if it was not for the unhappy fate of my truly amiable Sister and my kind Aunt. If you could with convenience purchase me and send by Thomas, 7½ yards of neat dark Silk, I would be glad to make the latter a present before she goes up the Country. The mail closes at 12 & I shall be obliged to close my scrawl that you may receive before T. leaves you. Write to me a long sweet kind good husband's letter to comfort me. My dear, my Precious Husband farewell. My Wedd. love, farewell

Your Devoted Jane

My Dear Husband   *Louisville, July 5th 1819*

I have I believe received all your letters that you have written to me since you left & one contained 20 Dollars. Your two of last few days mail found me well, but the two Boys but just recovered from dangerous illness. James had a fever for seven days without intermittence and it continued several Days and parts of days afterwards. . . . He is again on his feet & begins to look better. James is nearly well. On last friday on the receipt of your last I was well but know not from what cause but I do suppose the anxiety, violent agitation and distress of hearing of your danger fell into disturbed [sleep] & awakened in note a very violent palpitation but as usual attended with vomiting and in consequence bursted a vein and threw up a good deal of

Blood. I became alarmed and sent for the Doctor. . . . I was bled with some difficulty but when completed restored the disorderly action of the pulse & reduced the fever and to-day I am up writing to all in this life I hold dear to me. I could not help calling on my Dear Husband and I know you were thinking strongly on me. Nothing remains now but weakness. Cousin David was sick last week and is but just now recovered. He never closed his eyes the night I was so ill, and poor fellow, he was greatly alarmed at my illness. My sister, nurse to both and has a busy time. Aunt has not returned. I received a long letter last week from her & says she is much better, only as usual fostering her imagination about nothing.

Mrs. McCanlis has been removed to her daughter's in the country where she can be better attended to. Mrs. Martin's daughter who lives in this place, health is very bad and is totally disqualified for the duties of waiting so constantly on the old lady [who] labours under no particular disease, but nature appears to be wearing out. The rest of our friends in this place are all well. Uncle William never scarcely leaves us especially when any thing is the matter with us. I shall not close my letter until tomorrow. I have written much more than I expected I could have done when I began. It is now late and I got up since dinner. Farewell, my beloved, I shall conclude tomorrow [if] the Lord spares me life & health. The power of Almighty protect my adored husband and return him safe to my faithful and longing arms & throbbing heart. Tell Thomas my kind regards I send him & thanks for his good behavior in this last tryed instance. James is talking about and bragging every day of his brother, Thomas & Father & the mare pony & is continually talking of an indian lasso you are to bring him. If [you] see anything of wild Birds, bring me the feathers to make a fan, and your daughter, if we all live and are well when we meet, I think you will like a great deal. She is a fine, well grown and a good looking child, but not handsome. . . .

> *Your affectionate*
> *J. Green*

6th   This morning not well, but better & shall close this: I think I am not able to bear the exertion of writing any [more] though I have much to say. I feel greatly agitated & shall, I feel so until I hear from you. Pray write immediately on the receipt of this, it will in some measure relieve my agonies. I could fill up another sheet, but the mail closes at 12. I have no more time than to bid you adieu, my dear precious & let me hear as soon as possible from you.

> *July 12, 1819*

On hearing that my letter was not sent by the last mail, I had it sent for and on reading it over, I can not send you a better account of my late illness than contained in it. I however can say I think matters better, and none of the most alarming of the symptoms have occurred since I received yours written at Irwington & I greatly fear you will be disappointed in not receiving a letter owing to the stupidity of the post master [who] neglected putting my letter in the mail. I, however will hazard this, at any rate I'm afraid you will think hard and suppose me negligent and not sufficiently attentive to your letter not to send my letter to the place you expected. O grant this may out run you that you may see your poor wife's name once more. It is very feeble and a very indiffrent specimen of my feelings which overflows with tender sympathies all your anxiety, care, pains, perplexities, disappointments & difficulties. My little ones call of me so often that I scarcely get leave to finish a sentence. Only to think of James. I just told him to rock the cradle (as his sister was crying), he answered me very smartly to suckle her. He has this morning tied up a paper full of flowers for his father, and intends making up a paper for his Brother Thomas, and asks me every day if his <u>pa</u> & his Brother <u>Tos</u> (as he will call him) does not love him. Kollock begins to catch sounds and repeat them smartly but his ill health has made him very Backward and sometimes ill tempered, but in general very amiable. Ann is not so well, I think, but takes notice and I think can recognize her mother. I hope she will look like her half sister and resemble her in every fascination. I have much to say of such trifles that interest only a mother. I shall stop here and hope you will not be tried with my nothings & entreat all mighty to Bless and restore my husband safe to my arms and embrace. Bless and preserve you now and forever Amen

J. Green

My Dear Husband,   Louisville, August 25, 1819
   I feel considerable disappointment at not receiving a letter from you last Friday. I, however, suppose you could not travel so fast as you thought you could with James. I hope & trust you arrived safe without much fatigue. I have always accustomed James to have his head washed with soap & a brush once a week & wet and combed every day, this will prevent filth, though with a romping fellow like him, not sufficient to keep him neat. However this latter not very important, would be glad you would have the former strictly attended to. Kollock and Ann were both sick yesterday but are both better today. I gave each caster oil which acted very favourably and put them in flanel. David is better and writes to his mother today, will apprise her of your intention of sending for her in the way you mentioned to me & will anxiously wait her coming. I trust your business will go on satisfactorily and that I shall have the pleasure of seeing you shortly & if not necessary to leave my Darling Boy, shall feel much greater at seeing all the

Dear Absentees together. Grant I may not be disappointed, Father of Mercies, how natural to hope for everything good and a mark of divine goodness that is no sin, if it was I should be a great transgressor.

I enclosed six dollars to Mrs. Bettor to purchase linen cambrick. Would be glad to know if it was received the week before you visited this last as I am in immediate want of it and would be glad I could get it the first opportunity a good assortment of thread and needles of every number, I am without them & none to be had that is worth in this place. Flanel & a piece of good linen and a square of Bath Coating to make a nurse' shawl, the materials for making a quart of Paragorick & a bottle of Caster oil will perhaps be all that will be necessary for you to bring with you. A pair of our large Blankets, also. I do not like to bundle you up without it is convenient.

God of mercy bless and preserve my Dear husband & restore him safe to my arms. Be kind to my precious Boy and kiss him for me & remember me kindly to Thomas and accept my heart with all its affections, sympathies & regrets

Your own
J. Green

Louisville

My Dear Beloved,   *[Sept] 22, 1819*

Both your letters previous to your leaving Milledgeville came safe to hand, the money I returned to David & he, unfit as he was, is gone for his mother. They have outstayed their time & my poor sister is in great uneasiness of mind lest some accident has happened. Your Boys are much better likewise the little girl. . . . How rejoiced I feel at the prospect of seeing you at the time you mention & shall punctually write to you every week by the way you mentioned. Grant that my dear husband may get through his labours sooner than he contemplated when I saw him last. . . . Give my kind love to Thomas and receive the all of my heart. Bless you forever, my dear husband

           Your own J. Green

           Louisville
My Dear Husband,   *Nov. 16*

 Last week's letter not being sent to you occasioned me distress enough without not receiving one from you at the usual time. Uncle enquired of some persons that had seen you which relieved my mind as to your health & I hope that my not hearing directly from you may have originated in the same cause of your not hearing from me. The mail closes so early lately that mine was not sent soon enough, and ever since friday last I have been in one continual palpitation expecting you, yet I know [you] must have business to transact that may detain you there much longer than you expected. Still I know you were sick when you wrote last and I did fear you were much worse. While Col. Shellmore mentioned seeing you which set me more at rest on that score. However whatever cause it may have originated in, I hope it is now entirely removed & I shall hold you soon in my arms. I have an aching tooth which troubles me a good deal, otherwise tolerably well. James & Ann are fat and well & poor Koll, I have been giving him a worm medicine which I hope will be of great advantage to him. Today he is smart and chatters like a parrot, talks incessantly about Pa & his Brother Thomas. James is on the tiptoe of expectation. He has told and bragged to every one about your coming & all those fine things you have in the study until we are tired. You will excuse my stopping since my little ones demand my care & are always wanting my attention, this perhaps (you) need not be reminded of, therefore conclude with my kind regards to Thomas and prayers for your health and happiness, and remember my throbing heart is waiting for you

Your own J. Green

Jane Green died on December 12, 1828.

In 1821, after a public school was established in Milledgeville, William Green was appointed headmaster of the Baldwin County Academy, the first public school in the state.

In 1832, the year that Oliver Prince moved to Milledgeville, Virginia was seven years old. James Green, a handsome seventeen-year-old, could hardly have noticed such a youngster, but the two families apparently moved in the same social circles. In that year both Major Oliver H. Prince and the erudite Dr. William Montgomery Green appeared at a Temperance meeting banquet offering splendid toasts.

Educated by his father, James was being prepared for his chosen career as a doctor and surgeon by Dr. Benjamin A. White of Milledgeville. Having completed his preparatory course, he enrolled in Jefferson Medical College in Philadelphia. In 1837, upon graduation, he returned south to Macon where his father was now editor of the *Georgia Messenger* and entered into practice with his brother, Henry Kollock Green. Almost from the beginning their practice was varied and extensive, and James rose rapidly to prominence in the town.

Virginia, in 1837 only twelve years old and so recently bereaved, perhaps merely regarded the young doctor as a family friend. There were her studies to consider and she and her sister, Fanny, were carefully tutored in all the accomplishments of antebellum young ladies. There were lessons in French, elocution, composition, history, and geography, as well as needlework.

Later the girls were sent to Montpelier Institute, an Episcopal academy for young women, located on the Thomaston Road seventeen miles west of Macon. The academy was established in 1841 by Bishop Stephen Elliott, the first bishop of Georgia. Its attractive grounds were enhanced with natural springs of mineral water and wooded glens. During the summer months the area was also the site of a popular health resort. Bishop Elliott had labored hard to build the academy and used his own finances, and by 1843 it was beginning to flourish.

From there the fifteen-year-old Fanny wrote several letters to Virginia who had recently graduated from the academy and was visiting the Hillhouse relatives in Troy, New York.

Lamar Hall '43
Montpelier

My own <u>dear</u> Sister,   *June 1st*

I would have answered your welcome letter before but various things prevented, however, I will put it off no longer.

I really think, sister, that you are "<u>too</u> bad" to treat us all at home so, and myself in particular, when you had no good reason that I could think of—except that you had been to New York—and I am sure that pen, ink & paper are as plentiful in New York as in Troy. I expect you will be home in October—at least as soon as frost for Uncle Washington is afraid for you to come before that time—I am sure <u>I</u> shall be overjoyed to see you—for it seems now that I have no sister though I <u>often</u>, yes, often think of you. My holidays are over & I have returned to school. I remained at home in vacation which was the month of May, during that time I saw our <u>dear</u> brother only <u>three</u> times!! He traveled about a deal I expect that was the reason, his health is good, I believe.

I have not been well for a few days past, but am a deal better this afternoon.

The last time I heard from home, Cousin Sarah had been very sick. Aunt Selina was at that time very unwell & Grandmama was not as well as usual, all the rest are quite well I believe. I expect to go home in July, on the 4th perhaps. The Bishop has directed that we all should write on unruled paper. I cannot write <u>very</u> straight, so I thought it proper to adopt lines in writing such a <u>particular</u> letter as this, though I <u>generally</u> do without. I am doing very well in all my studies, and also in <u>French</u>, do not be surprised if <u>in the course of time</u> you receive a French letter from me, though to be sure it will be "in the course of time." When was the last time you heard from <u>dear</u> Mrs. Belcher? I answered her last letter an <u>age</u> ago—but she has not written to me since. I have received a letter from Mrs. Clark & Clifford since I wrote to you last, but have answered neither. When I spoke of Mrs. Fay's baby, I meant Mrs. Howard Fay's. It was baptized when the Bishop was here and is called Susan Elliott. Did you receive a sermon of the Bishop's that I sent you? I could not then well write. It was on the Foxes, the little Foxes, I cannot repeat the rest but it is in Song of Soloman L. 15. I hope you got it. I think I have written a pretty long letter so I will close in a few minutes. I should have been delighted to accompany you to that Opera you speak of but I should not have been able to understand a word of it. You cannot think how I long to go where I can <u>see</u> something. I perfectly <u>envy</u> you though to sure you do not see much. Do you ever go to theatres? What would you say if I were to go on in January, though I have not the <u>least</u> idea of it at present. Our school has enlarged so, we have fifty-one scholars now including Mrs. Fay's two daughters, Mrs. Parey's, one and one of Mrs. Campbells. We have five teachers. Cousin Mary does not come now, she has stopped & is going to school in Forsyth. You cannot imagine how much curiosity I have to see Cousin Charlotte Buel, and if you can in your next do send a little specimen of her writing to satisfy it. Mary Virginia *writes a very pretty hand for a child of her age and intends writing to me. Mary Prince writes well enough also. Well, dear sister, I must close. All I am sure would send love if they knew I were writing. So good bye*

> *Your devoted sister*
> *Fanny*

Fanny continued her correspondence to her sister from Montpelier Academy in the summer of 1844. By this time, Virginia had returned to Macon.

Dear Sister,   *June 12, 1844*

Notwithstanding my resolution of not writing to you again, I feel myself almost compelled to do so on account of the <u>small</u> number of my correspondents, all of whom now, I believe, owe me a letter with the exception of yourself. I do wish you would, if you <u>can</u> that is, find Blairs Lectures, as I believe we will commence it when Mrs. Parey returns which will be about the 1st of July, or the last of June, at or before which time Mrs. Roberts & Miss Toley will depart, the former for England & the latter "Home." You have heard of Mrs. Coley, a new teacher we have for <u>this</u> term only. She is an English lady, but resides (I believe) in Savannah. She teaches music & drawing, understands <u>French</u> perfectly, has two children, one of them is here, a little girl about eleven years of age. I have not seen much of her yet, but what I have seen I like very much. Our school hours are altered from what they were last term. We commence in the morning at eight & dismiss at twelve, in the evening at three, dismiss at five. It is much pleasanter to do I think than to have the six hours equally divided, besides it gives me a little time for a <u>nap</u> now & then before evening school.

It has been very warm lately & we have been very much annoyed by bugs, large black <u>bugs</u> which bite dreadfully & then there are such numbers of them too. So many that Mr.

Fay has often had large fires made round the house to attract them from it. Today has been quite cool & even in the middle of the day we had little sunshine, heard one or two of the young ladies express their opinions on the subject by saying "they wished all the summer was just so" I wish you would tell me in your next, whether you & Aunt & Uncle think it necessary for me to study "Logic," don't forget to tell me & above all things dont leave it to me. It would be a great pleasure, indeed, to write to dear M. C. C., but there is one thing which prevents, especially as she wishes me to write on one particular subject. Perhaps you know what it is, if you do, do tell her the reason of my silence.

Very few new scholars have entered this term, all, or nearly all the old ones have returned & I hear that a great many applications have been made, & a number, too are waiting to fill up any vacancy which may occur. We have had one addition to our bedroom, which makes eight., the last has not yet arrived, expected every day. I wish you would send me my instruction book, if you can get it from Uncle S's. How is Miss F. M. P.'s health at present? It was not very good when I left town. Poor Grandmother, how does she stand the loss of her little pet. I feared it would have some influence on her health. Anne Tracy says she intends sending you a "long message" the next time I write, but for the present will you accept her love. Give my best love to all at home & do you write to me often & not such little pigmies of notes as the one I last received, but long letters. How do you do now?, for my part I cant see how you can get along at all without me, now that Miss C. is absent & I dare say when I return I shall see you looking as pale & thin as you did when you came from Troy. If you see any of my "young friends" in Macon as Miss Anne T. called Sarah's friends, remember me affectionately to them. I was very sorry to hear you speak thus concerning my visit to New York next summer. I really think I deserve it after being cooped up here for more than three years, besides you promised to bring on "our youngest" at some future time & I think next summer will be as good a time as any, but never mind, we'll see about it. Adieu once more, my affectionate

love to all,
Your sincerely attached
Sister

[July 17, 1844]
Lamar Hall
Dear Sister,   *Montpelier*

I was much disappointed on last Tuesday, not to receive a note or letter from you by Elbert, especially as I much needed the articles that I sent for & I was very anxious to hear also when you expected Uncle and Aunt home.

I think they will let me go down, when they come.

Mrs. Parey has not yet arrived. She was expected in the Great Western, but it has come without her & we do not know now how long it will be before she will leave England. She expected to sail first, I believe, on the 4th June. Mrs. Roberts & Miss Toley have gone & we have only two teachers to take charge of the school, Miss Bush, & Mrs. Coley. Mr. Fay, Mrs. Shellman, Anna Marie & Hal left Montpelier for Meriwether last Friday. Neither of the girls was in very good health; & they are to remain two months, I believe.

Meta has been sick for a little while but has now entirely recovered, except from the effects of the mustard plaster on her forehead, which has blistered a little.

Yesterday was the 16th! did you forget darling Walley, or did you not think of him ofter during the day, as I did? And Aunt and Uncle also, how queer that they should all three be absent on their birthdays. You have not written to me in a long time. Do write soon & let me know <u>all</u> about <u>everything</u>. When you receive this do write <u>immediately</u> & tell me if you think there is any probability of my paying *you a short visit either before or after Uncle returns. If there is not, do follow the directions I am about to give. Get me something, I don't care what, whether a book or any other little "Jim-crack" only let it be suitable for a birthday present I wish to give one of the girls.*

If you think that there is any probability of my coming down, don't get it, but write & tell me as I am very anxious for this: I will tell you whether to get it or not in my next. I wrote to Clifford a week or two ago. She has not answered my letter, as soon as she does I will send it to you. I wish you would send me one of Charlotte's letters. I love to read them so & I will take care of it, a funny one, do. If you have anything to send me, just have it left at Scotts & Casharts & it will be brought up by the first opportunity. Do send me some Maccassar oil or Cassada, I had rather have the latter. Do send it, my hair is in such a state, you cannot imagine. I should like some powder, too & some handkerchiefs. I have something funny to tell you when I get home, that is, if you can keep a secret. I don't believe you can, for I have tried you once or twice.

We have an abundance of peaches now, clear stone the cling stone have not yet opened. I hope you have as many as you want. I took a very pleasant bath today, both plunge & shower bath & take one almost every week.

I have learnt lately to play chess, I like it very much more than I even do Back-gammon, from which I am pretty much wearied. You know practice makes perfect & I hope by the time I come home I shall be able to play with you or Uncle. Meta is quite well, thank you and sends her love to you. She received a letter from Kate a week or two ago. Much obliged for the candy, very nice indeed. You have not written me a real long letter this term. I long to receive one, as Charlotte calls it in "your own round distinct hand writing" & I do hope that my wish will be granted by the next mail. My love to Miss Mary Cumming when you write to her. (you see I never forget to send my love to those who have been so kind as to send theirs to me) & tell her that I will embrace the first opportunity that is presented to answer her kind note.

I have sent by Mrs. Roberts to New York for some purse twist. I hope to learn how to nett & knit, both. Do you continue to take charge of my Picciola now?, do not, I pray you, neglect it. If you please, send me what I have written for, particularly the oil, I do indeed need it very much. Give my love to Grandmother, Aunt, Cousin Sarah, Brother & all the children. If you have received a letter from Uncle or Aunt, do send it to me.

Adieu, dear Sister, write soon, do & discharge all the commissions of your ever aff. & devoted

Fanny

According to the custom of the period, when Virginia Prince and Dr. James Mercer Green were married a contract was written by Washington Poe for his niece and ward. She was considered wealthy, "possessing certain properties both real and personal of lands, negroes, notes of hand, Rail Road Stock and other articles." This property, left by Oliver Prince (though Virginia inherited only one-third of his estate), was so large that it provided well for her and her descendants through two generations. The marriage, especially during the prewar years, was a happy one. Dr. Green, a warmhearted, compassionate man, particularly loved children and animals, sometimes keeping a small puppy or kitten in his dressing gown pocket. He was an earnest, hard worker in his numerous and exacting professional duties, and active in many political and charitable causes in Macon.

Dr. Green was the first to suggest the establishment of an institution for the blind in Macon. In 1851, he received a letter from Dr. Robley Dunglison, his former tutor and a trustee of the Pennsylvania Institution for the Blind, brought by Walter S. Fortescue, a highly educated blind young man. Fortescue, wishing to establish a school for the blind in Georgia, had been told by Dr. Dunglison that the Drs. Green in Macon—Kollock also practiced there—could be of invaluable assistance. James and his brother cordially welcomed Fortescue.

James, in particular, eagerly promoted the idea that the school should be established in Macon. He immediately became a leading spirit in the effort and enlisted the help of many prominent citizens. In April 1851 a meeting was announced in the Macon paper "for the purpose of encouraging and sustaining an effort for the commencement of an Institution for the education of the blind youth of our State." At the meeting Dr. Green was appointed a member of the temporary board of trustees of the Georgia Academy for the Blind, and later when the board was reorganized, he became its president in 1852, an office he held for nearly thirty years.

In its early years the institution had many troubles, not the least of which was Fortescue himself, as extant letters to Dr. Green from Dr. Dunglison disclose.

Philadelphia

My Dear Sir,   *June 7, 1851*

I have been greatly embarrassed as to my course of procedure in regard to the money to be drawn by Mr. Fortescue. He had presented me with an amount of articles required, made up for him by Mr. Chapin, the principal of our Institution which appears to me to be correct and advisable.

I have no vouchers formerly paid, and some of the articles I told Mr. Chapin—printed in our Institution—were to be presented to you without charge. These and other articles amount to about 160 dollars.—A sum which could be reduced by the deduction in question.

I have not deemed it proper, therefore, to give Mr. Fortescue the power of drawing upon me for <u>two hundred</u>

<u>dollars</u>, but told him to have the bills sent to the principal of our Institution and I will pay them after which I can draw upon you for the amount expended. As a member of the Committee of Instructors of our Board of Managers, I told Mr. Chapin yesterday that our contributions to you must be gratuitous.

Fortescue was a little startled at my decision; but he was perfectly satisfied when I explained to him that as a business man such a course was indispensable and I had the less hesitation in adopting it as on Thursday last the Board of Managers awarded him the sum of $150 as an old pupil which I paid him yesterday. I need hardly say to you that he has great self respect, but will require that he should be subjected to some control. I am preparing a card of business for the Board of Managers and when completed, I will send it to you by mail, if it can be received, which I suppose it can. You will see that it will facilitate business at our meetings greatly. Fortescue will bring with him a copy of our Constitution & regulations. The times of meetings, you will see by the card, has been greatly altered. Fortescue proposes leaving here for Georgia on Monday.

Truly yours
Robley Dunglison

Philadelphia
Aug. 30, 1851

My dear Sir,

Mr. Chapin has presented to me this day the accompanying amount of one hundred & sixty-five dollars & seven cents, and vouchers, which—as he was in want of the money—I have paid him.

I would have drawn upon you for the sum, but I have thought it might be more easy for you to send a draft from one of your banks on a bank here, and moreover, I was ignorant of the exact form for a draft if I drew one upon you.

Whatever course you may adopt will be satisfactory to me. I trust that your announcement has been propitious.

Mr. Chapin tells me that he had received a newspaper which mentioned the initial steps you had taken.

I have recently returned from a short sojourn in the mountainous regions of Connecticut, a new country home, and one full of interest.

> *Believe me, my dear Sir*
> *Truly yours*
> *Robley Dunglison*

Dr. Dunglison, a supporter of both the Georgia Academy for the Blind and Dr. Green, sent in 1853 a black-bordered letter of condolence to his Macon friend, who had recently lost two children.

> *Philadelphia*
> *Nov. 3, 1853*

My Dear Sir:

I was greatly distressed by the receipt of your letter informing me of the additional bereavement you had experienced and the anxiety to which you had been subjected on account of the illness of Mrs. Green.

Be assured, my dear Sir, that you have my sincere sympathy and my congratulations that her health has been restored. Your own, I regret to learn, has not been progressively improving as I had been led to hope it was.

Richard is returned & is re-established. He had fallen off in his nutrition in the Spring, and especially at a time when I could not bestow much attention on him. He improved, however, after this, but in June became exceedingly thin and pale, and I determined he should experience a complete change in the physical and moral circumstances surrounding him. The voyage affected almost everything, and he has been, and is, entirely well. He is now fit & is attending lectures; and I shall endeavor to prevent him from too close application.

I thank you much for your kind invitation that he should visit you at Macon, and sojourn with you in Florida. I hope that it will not be necessary for him to leave Philadelphia, but should he be, there are none to which I could send him, in whose care and attention I should repose more confidence than in you and yours.

I regret I did not see your brother on his return, but am glad to find he experienced benefit from his Northern sojourn as I felt certain he could.

As for your Principal, after what has occurred, too much confidence ought not be placed in his ingenuousness. It was stated positively to the Principal of our Institution that the two were offered a certain salary per year, but they were willing to stay with us if their salaries were increased. Against this I strongly set my feeling, and under all the circumstances preferred to part with them.

Willie and Richard desire their kindest regards to you and believe me

> *My dear Sir*
> *Truly yours*
> *Robley Dunglison*

Although Fortescue served as principal of the academy during the struggling years of 1851–53, he was, understandably, soon replaced. Dr. Green's long and devoted efforts in behalf of the Georgia Academy for the Blind were recorded by the *Macon Telegraph* in 1881:

Dr. James Mercer Green, although at that time, actively engaged in the duties of his profession and encumbered with a large practice, found time to exert all the influence he had, enlisting his numerous friends by personal appeals and solicitations in behalf of the enterprise. Preliminary meetings of the citizens were called to consider the matter, before which he appeared with Mr. Fortescue, and by his intelligent and zealous influence, a temporary organization was formed for the purpose of taking subscriptions, he and his friends, through his agency, contributing largely to the funds raised. . . .

He was from his universally acknowledged fitness for the position by a unanimous vote of his associates appointed attending physician of the academy, and in that position fully merited and retained, throughout this long period, the entire confidence of the trustees and officers charged with the internal management of the establishment. To the duties of this office, always varied and often perplexing, he gave the most unremitting and assiduous attention, and they were discharged not only with scrupulous fidelity, but with the highest skill. He had the highest regard for his responsibilities in the offices he held; and in the discharge of the various duties they imposed, he displayed eminent qualifications and fitness, great zeal, activity and talent. His connection with the Academy for the Blind will be long and gratefully remembered by its friends and the people of the State.

The house on Poplar Street that the Greens purchased in 1858 was not their first. With a $2000 down payment (from her father's estate money), Virginia Prince Green bought a house in November 1846. There their first child, Mary Raymond, was born on January 16, 1847. They were not to enjoy the home for long, however, as on May 1, 1848, Dr. Green noted in his journal that the house had been destroyed by fire.

For the next ten years they owned and lived in two other homes, each successively lost by the disastrous fires that often occurred during this period. Between these calamities they boarded in various homes throughout the city. In one (the Day house, home of Mary Day, who later married Sidney Lanier), a son—named for William Montgomery Green—was born on August 19, 1851, and died on March 15, 1853.

Although the Greens by this time were the parents of three other children, the tragedy had such a devastating effect that they soon moved to the home of Mrs. Mark D. Clark's (Virginia's Aunt Nancy) where a girl, Frances, was born May 17, 1853. This child lived for only five months, dying at Washington Poe's home in October.

After the birth of their sixth child, Selina Virginia, on July 9, 1855, Dr. Green noted briefly in his journal that in May of 1857 he was "burnt out 3rd time." It is not surprising, then, to see his final entry: "May 18, 1858, moved to Powers house (brick)."

It was their fourth and final home, and was to remain in the Green family and their descendants' possession for the next seventy-four years. Like Prince's home in Milledgeville, it is listed on the National Register of Historic Buildings and pictured and described in many architectural books. But unlike Rockwell its construction date is documented.

Built in 1840 by Ambrose Chapman on a half acre lot on the then fashionable Poplar Street, its architecture was a modification of the Federal style. Chapman obtained the lot from the mayor and council of Macon for $405 and signed a lease for 999 years "paying one peppercorn on the first day of April each year (if demanded)." The deed, signed by Mayor Washington Poe, was drawn up January 13, 1841, Chapman previously having had a bond for title.

Seventeen days after the signing of the deed Ambrose Chapman sold the house to Henry G. Lamar for $8000. On August 1, 1846, the Lamar estate sold the property to Judge Abner Powers, who twelve years later sold the handsome home to the Greens.

Brick homes were a rarity in the area during this period due to the abundance of wood available. Of elegant yet simple design, the house has twelve-inch-thick exterior and interior walls built of handmade bricks. Marble steps flanked by ornamental railings lead to a portico supported

Chapman-Green-Poe House, Macon.
Home of Virginia and James Mercer Green.
Photograph by Ken Hill.

with cast-iron columns. Matching cast-iron work tops the roof of the stoop and forms a balcony across the entire front of the second floor. While the front of the house facing the street once gave the appearance of only two stories, a rear view shows three. The basement was used for dining as well as Dr. Green's office. In the rear stood a kitchen, the coach house, and servants' quarters.

Inside the "L"-shaped interior, with one vast room on the right and two equally large rooms to the left, the front hall ends in a curved wall at the rear. A freestanding elliptical stairway leads to the upper floor where the rooms were arranged like those on the lower.

In this house the Greens lived for the remaining years of their lives. Here, too, their last child, a son, was born on August 21, 1861. On that date, his father wrote in the family Bible: "James Edward Beauregard Green was born on Wednesday the 21st day of August 1861 at 3½ P.M. just one month after the great Battle of Manassas."

The Civil War had begun and Dr. Green, though overage, volunteered. On February 5, 1862, he was appointed surgeon in the Medical Department of the Confederate Army and was sent to Richmond. He served in Virginia until January 17, 1863, when he was appointed surgeon in charge of the four hospitals in Macon. Under Dr. Green's direction these hospitals won approval for their neat appearance and cleanliness.

But during the latter days of the war, when thousands of wounded soldiers were being brought to the Confederate hospitals in Macon, additional space was sorely needed. Prevented by court action from taking possession of a hotel and college in Macon for hospital purposes, Dr. Green gave voice to impatient and harsh words. In a report to the state hospital director, he wrote: "I want these people to have some little of the burdens of the war, as well as all its profits. It is disgusting to see the contemptuous indifference & even hatred that many of these wealthy foreigners

& Yankees & some disloyal men of Southern birth have to everything concerning the soldiers, Hospitals, etc. I desire most sincerely to teach some of these men their duties to the Govt. that protects them."

James Mercer Green died on June 13, 1881. In the *Macon Telegraph*'s obituary he was praised as *"one of the most prominent, useful, distinguished and highly esteemed citizens of the city."* Continuing, the newspaper noted: *"Dr. Green had very exalted but very just views of the character and learning of his profession. . . . The foundation of all professional excellence is broad, generous, and extensive culture, and Dr. Green was a conspicuous example of this truth. He was well read in history, philosophy, and polite literature. His acquaintance with the best of our English classics was extensive and accurate."*

His funeral was held in Christ Church (Episcopal), of which he was a longtime member, and he was buried in the Green plot at Rose Hill Cemetery.

Virginia lived on into the early part of the twentieth century. At her death on December 12, 1905, she was survived by only two of her seven children, Edward and Selina Virginia. On February 12, 1882, the daughter—called Lina by her family and friends—became the wife of Washington Poe's youngest son, William.

Elizabeth Frances Prince—
James Roswell King

Elizabeth Frances Prince was married on April 17, 1851, to James Roswell King of Roswell, Georgia. James's grandfather, Roswell King, who was born May 3, 1765, in Windsor, Connecticut, had served as a private in the Revolutionary War and later moved to Georgia, settling in Darien. On April 14, 1792, he married Catherine Barrington, daughter of Josiah Barrington, a kinsman of James Edward Oglethorpe. Fort Barrington on the Altamaha River in Georgia, an outpost built before the Revolution for defense against the Spaniards, was named for him.

Roswell King, a man of great energy and enterprise, established a prospering business dealing in lumber, cotton, and rice in Darien shortly before 1800. For a number of years he supervised the vast Georgia plantations of Pierce Butler, whose wife, the English actress Fanny Kemble, wrote a blistering attack on the slave conditions there. Her book, *Journal of a Residence on a Georgian Plantation in 1838–1839*, was said to have been one of the causes of England's rejection of the South during the Civil War.

In 1828, King made a trip to the North Georgia gold mining regions on business for the Darien Bank. Passing through the wild beautiful area of the foothills of the mountains he noted the fertile land and fine water of the Chattahoochee River. Later he returned with his son Barrington, and together they purchased large tracts of land, some from the Indians, and established the village of Roswell. As an inducement to other settlers of this town, he offered free land to a group of his friends from Darien. Together the father and son laid out the plan of the town with wide streets and a park, and donated building sites for an academy and two churches. Here the Kings organized a cotton mill in 1839, and soon the village was the scene of much activity. Handsome homes were built by six coastal families, and a settlement of brick dwellings was constructed for the workers of the Roswell Manufacturing Company, said to be the first brick apartment houses in the state. Later Barrington King built the Ivy Woolen Mill, and Roswell became an important industrial town.

The beautiful Greek Revival mansion that Barrington King began to build for his family in 1839 required five years to complete. It was located on six wooded acres on a slight rise overlooking the town. The architect, Willis Ball of Connecticut, had virgin timber cut and seasoned for two years before construction was begun. After the house was completed and named Barrington Hall, the grounds and gardens were designed by an English landscape gardener.

It was to this home that James Roswell King brought his new bride, Fanny, in 1851. Their wedding trip, a visit to Judge Buel and his family in Troy, New York, had extended through many weeks of the summer.

Roswell, populated by the cultured, aristocratic families from the coast, welcomed the pretty blonde bride from Macon. Fanny, who had been well educated under the supervision of her guardian, Washington Poe, became a member of the Presbyterian church in which James was an elder. There she was active in the newly organized Ladies Missionary Society and was elected its first president, an office she held for almost thirty years.

Fanny's life for the next ten years was, not unlike many other lives in the small village of Roswell, full of great joy as well as much sorrow. Her first-born child, a girl who Fanny named for the well-loved cousin in Troy, Hariett Buel, died at Virginia's "house on the hill" in Macon. She was four years old.

Elizabeth Frances Prince King.
Portrait dated 1851. Artist unknown.
Photograph by J. Carol Gore.

James Roswell King.
*Photograph taken by the Wenderoth, Taylor & Brown studio of Philadelphia
after the Civil War.*

Barrington Hall, Roswell.
Home of Fanny and James Roswell King.

A letter written to her sister in Macon just one month past the start of hostilities between the North and South was a mixture of elation and foreboding. The "Brother Tom" whom Fanny wrote of so glowingly was James's brother, Thomas Edward King, who was soon to see action at Manassas.[3]

My dear Sister   *Roswell, May 29, 1861*

I have just returned from witnessing the most heart rending & at the same time the noblest sight I have ever seen— our volunteers, the "Roswell Guard" left today for Atlanta, they form a part of Gartrell's regiment & will be sent to Richmond on Saturday, they form a fine company of upwards of 90 men & in their uniforms, with bands playing and colors flying they are a stirring sight. Brother Tom will, in all probability be their Capt & they are perfectly enthusiastic about him, quantities join in the mere hope of having him for their Capt. I have been busy day and night since I received Dr's letter about the slippers—I am very sorry to hear you have been so sick but I hope it is over now, I wish I could come & see you; I am going down to Atlanta Friday & see our soldiers off. He could not buy anything to make a flag in Atlanta or in Marietta, so I cut up my crimson crape shawl & Marie supplied white satin & blue silk from two of her dresses & we made a beautiful flag with "R.G" in big white silk letters & eleven silken stars on a blue silk field formed our Union. James made a handsome staff & mother took off the blue silk tassels of her dressing gown, so altogether we got up a pretty flag. J—[James] presented it in our name & Mr. Chas. Dunwody, Lieut—, responded, it was very exciting, Oh! to see the poor wives & mothers cling round their husbands & sons—as if they could not be torn apart & to hear the piteous wail that went up as they were hurried away from them was distressing. The company is a very fine one, not a man among it but is a splendid marksman tho' of course they are not drilled well yet, but under a good Capt., one they love, one they doat on as they do Tom they will make splendid soldiers.

We made them everything we could think of, the Ladies have worked faithfully & I feel as if I could give up every-thing I have to help our country in this time of need. I have no doubt my husband will have to go after a while if this war continues & I hear that the best judges say it must last for years yet. I think it would be better for him to stay at home to help them by keeping his Factory going but they cannot use their judgment when their feelings & resent-ment are so roused. Ralph's wife & Mrs. Adams have both been helping to work for our soldiers. I feel sorry for them both, tho' I try & hold back when I am with them from abusing the "Yankees."

But despite the early excitement, the summer of 1864 was the beginning of the end for Georgia. All through the war the Ivy Woolen Mill, which James, his father, and brother operated, had produced the cloth (called Roswell grey) for Confederate uniforms. Sherman's army was advancing closer to Roswell, and the Kings knew that the destruction of their mills would be the Federal's prime objective. To save perhaps not both mills but at least the Ivy one, they hastily devised a plan. Thinking quickly, the owners transferred an interest in the mill to a French employee, a skilled weaver named Theophile Roche. When Union General Kenner Garrard with a unit of Sherman's army entered Roswell, he saw to his dismay the French flag flying over the mill.

To destroy property of the French government, Garrard knew, would cause an international incident. After writing for advice from General Sherman, Garrard received a long letter from him stating, "I had no idea that the factories in Roswell remained in operation . . . the utter distruction is right and meets with my entire approval, and to make the matter complete you will arrest the owners and employees, and send them under guard, charged with treason, to Marietta—and I will see to any man in America hoisting the French flag and then devoting his labor and capital to supplying armies in open hostility to our Government, and claiming the benefit of his neutral flag. Should you, under impulse of anger, natural at contemplating such perfidy, hang the wretch, I approve the act before hand."[5]

The Kings were not hanged and there is no record of their arrest, but the burning of his mill in July, 1864, aroused in James Roswell King such anger that shortly afterward he organized a company of men, equipped them at his own expense, and went with them as their captain to fight in the last bitter months of the war. Roswell was evacuated, and Fanny and her children took refuge in Macon in the home of Virginia and James Green.

The Greens's oldest son, sixteen-year-old Harry, only days before had answered Governor Joseph E. Brown's plea for all citizens of Macon who possessed a gun to volunteer for service. Harry was sent to fight in the area south of Atlanta and wrote home in the fall telling of his experiences there.

> On picket −2½ mi. from Camps
> My Dearest Mother,   26th Sept 1864
>
> I wrote you a letter sometime ago & have not received an answer. My Dear Mother, I began this letter the day before yesterday but circumstances have prevented me from finishing it until now. The whole Brigade passed our post yesterday on their way <u>to try to</u> capture a wagon train & several couriers have passed today with prisoners who report the whole command are engaged with the Yankees who <u>guard</u> the train & they say the Roswell Battalion stand it well. I would like very much to be with them. I have spoken to a few of them, they report themselves as tired of the war & when relieved they say they intend to go home & fight no more. You know that <u>is the old</u> tale which they all tell.
>
> I'm sorry to hear of the death of Joanna's little baby I

know it must be a sore loss to her & I sympathize with her very deeply.

30th My Dear Mother—so many accidents have happened since I commenced this letter that it looks like a series of disconnected sentences. The Roswell Batt. went through the fight as well or better then any of the rest of the troops. I am very sorry I was not in it, but was prevented by being on picket—I send this letter by George Gann of Co. A who was wounded in the little fight. He will bring you this letter to the house & he would be very much complemented if you asked him to dinner. I lost your interesting letter before I had hardly read it through. I wish you would write me just such another letter that I may be able to answer it in the way it ought to be. You spoke about my shoes being worn, they are very little worn & will last me this winter & I think all next summer as I have very little walking to do. I liked to have swapped my shoes for a pair of Yankee boots to a man who had a pair, which were too small for him, but I went 'round to see the man & he had taken his boots & split them in front so as to get them on & consequently had ruined them. How is the little foal getting along? I hope it is in good health. Please ask Hilly to take my gun & give it a good rub with a greased rag every week as I would not have it to become badly rusty for anything. How is Edward? I hope he is as fat as ever & says as many smart things. I wish you would write me some of things he says now & then. Have you got as many chickens as you used to have? The place where I first dated my letter at, was an old church called Flat Shoals church; it is in a beautiful situation with large oaks & hickory trees standing all around it—I passed a very pleasant time there & had a very good place to sleep at; in the Pulpit. You may think it was a very strange place to sleep in but notwithstanding, it was a very nice place. I send Sissy those little pieces of glass which I promised in one of my letters. My teeth are in a very bad fix & need plugging badly. I can hardly chew with *them. My India Rubber blanket is of a great deal of use to me when it rains as I keep perfectly dry when every body else is drenchingly wet. I have not had occasion to spend a cent of the specie you gave me. I forgot to tell you that at Flat Shoals, we came to within five miles of Lovejoys Station. I am afraid that I will not be able to answer Sissy's letter this time as George will leave directly. We will all draw woolen clothes & cotton underclothes in a week. Good bye my dear Mother*

    I am as ever your aff' son

Harry

Harry came home from the war unharmed, but died very young, at the age of twenty-six. At the end of the war, Fanny and James returned to Roswell. Barrington Hall had escaped destruction, but the mills, which were their livelihood, were in ruins. James, hoping to find employment, joined his brother Ralph in New York, where the family lived for four years.

In 1868, Fanny, ever cheerful, wrote from Brooklyn to Virginia:

My dear Sister,   *Brooklyn, Dec. 28, 1868*
    I am sorry to think that a Christmas has come and gone without sending you a letter from me. I hope you have thought as much of us as we have of you. The children as usual have spent a "very Merry Christmas"—children are so light hearted naturally that they enjoy <u>anything</u>, but really there was a great deal done this time to make it pleasant to them. Dr. Van Dyke's church had a Christmas tree for the two Sunday Schools connected with it, containing about 500 scholars and really it was quite an elegant affair. Then they had an evening entertainment and also a tree at Mrs. Harvey's (Fanny's school) so the children had a very pleasant time and it was pleasant to us too. We have never had such pleasant relations with any church (except in

Roswell) as we have with Dr. Van Dyke's. The people and pastor are <u>most cordial</u> to us, and in this land of enemies it is very pleasant and grateful to us.

We all miss dear Mamie very much. She was with us last year and added very much to our enjoyment. The children say constantly, "I wish Cousin Mamie was here." I have no Rebecca now to spoil the day and I hope I never shall again. I would rather be worse served and have some control of my household than to have anyone like her. Mamie knows. I long to see you all, I think of Dear Aunt Nancy, and long to hear from her, but we never do, and I can't say I deserve any better treatment; but you must give my best love to her and to Aunt Selina and tell them so.

I was very much disappointed about Eddy, I had hoped to have a visit from him as he came through New York, but I suppose the poor fellow was homesick and wanted to get away from this sloppy country as soon as he could. I do not blame him, it is a miserable cold climate.

I have been intending to send you and Aunt Selina a nice jar of Pineapple preserves in return for the treat of figs and peaches you two sent me by Eddy, but I have not seen a pineapple in [the] market since. But don't despair, I've got the jars safe and I will do it sometimes if all the greenbacks don't give out.

Tell Mamie her little chair is securely kept locked up in my closet. I don't allow anyone to touch it, and she shall have it if I can send it in April. Please tell her also that Mother has found her "Arctics" and will send to her by some opportunity. I am sorry it will be out of my power to come South this Spring. Since I weaned Marian we are both so much better that there is no excuse, but, my dear Sister, if we don't get on better than we are doing now, we will be obliged to give up this house and go <u>somewhere</u> where we can "make a living" and of course we would rather come South, than go anywhere else.

I wish you would write me a long nice letter like you used to, and tell me all about your chickens and pigs and the calf you are fattening up, and all your household affairs. You went and had your house nicely painted, Jimmy says, and never told me a word of it, till he came and saw it.

All send love and a Happy New Year to you all. We are expecting Henry Pratt, his wife and four children to stay with us a few days before they sail to South America to enter upon a mission at Bogota, so we will be pretty full— seventeen in family.

> *Good-bye,*
> *Your aff'*
> *Sister*

I send you a handkerchief for a token gift and a needle case for Mary.

Later the Kings returned to Roswell, where James assisted his family in rebuilding the mills, but a severe economic depression forced them into selling the property in the 1870's. Fanny died on January 5, 1881, after a lingering and painful illness of sixteen months. She was survived by her husband and six of her ten children.

Her husband wrote a touching memoir of her, published in Atlanta in 1881, dedicating the book "to the memory of a most affectionate wife from whom in God's providence I have been called to part." After describing her background and family history, James continued:

In person Mrs. King was short and stout. In complexion she was a blond with bright blue eyes and brown curling hair, having a handsome face, with perfectly chiseled lips, well formed brow and head, with the rich mellow voice and pleasant address for which the women of the South are so justly celebrated. Having received a good education, and being blessed with a retentive memory, she was esteemed a good judge of literature. She was also a very pleasant and impressive reader. So entertaining, in fact, were her readings, that both young and old found ample evening entertainment at home. In a married life of nearly thirty years, her husband never had occasion to seek any other society than the home circle for pleasure and diversion, and he has steadfastly refused to join any other organization than the church, because such would deprive him of a portion of his evenings at home.

Mrs. King had always enjoyed remarkable good health until she was stricken in September 1879, by the disease which terminated her life. She remained very much indisposed but never alarmingly sick until the following April when she went to Macon to consult her brother-in-law, Dr. James Mercer Green, at which time she had the first alarming attack. . . .

She was able to enjoy driving out nearly every day for four or five weeks. Being a great admirer of nature, one who found books in running brooks, sermons in stones, and beauty in everything, she had the greatest enjoyment in those autumn days, watching the ever varying hues of the fading and gently falling autumnal leaves, a sad though true emblem of her own precious life. There was no improvement during this time, the unrelenting disease held its course, not yielding to any treatment.

Concluding with an account of their devotions and discussions, he recollected the effects of Fanny's Christian faith and grace:

The last six weeks of her life was spent in great personal suffering. As her strong constitution yielded to disease, how beautifully was fulfilled the scripture "As the outward man perishes, the inward man is renewed day by day." . . . On retiring Monday night, she said "It will not be long," and desired me to read many precious promises from the Bible, and to sing the hymn: "Just as I am. . . ." She left messages of the most affectionate regard for her much loved Sister, the dear Doctor, aunt Nancy, and all friends. . . . She repeated in a strong voice again and again which gradually sank into a whisper: "Simply to Thy Cross I cling. Simply—cross—cling." . . . While sitting up, supported on either side, she breathed her life gently away, without a struggle.

During her final day and night, King noted in the memoir, Fanny

was gently waited on by my sister, Mrs. Baker, and one of our old family servants, Maum Zabbet, who had been called in to see how "Miss Fanny" was, and remained with her to the end, esteeming it a great privilege, as she said, to "wait on Miss Fanny."

James Roswell King died in Atlanta on January 27, 1897, and was buried in the Presbyterian cemetery in Roswell.

Epilogue

Prince's son, Oliver Jr., was educated at Yale and Princeton. Though not an especially good student, he showed a keen intellect and inherited his father's polished wit. He was admitted to the bar, and in 1845 purchased the *Macon Telegraph*. As editor of the newspaper, he advocated the advancement of the farmer, public education, and women's property rights. He wrote that Georgia capital should be invested in the state, and railed at the people for being "infatuated with cotton" and pleaded for the diversification of crops. He fought as a second lieutenant in the war with Mexico, and as a lieutenant-colonel in the Confederate Army he was aide-de-camp to General Howell Cobb. On June 15, 1852, he married Sarah M. R. Jackson, youngest daughter of Henry Jackson. At the comparatively early age of fifty-two, he died at Decatur, where he lived in retirement after the Civil War. He was buried in Athens, Georgia.

When Oliver Prince planned his trip to Boston to superintend the printing of the second edition of his digest, he had been asked by the trustees of Franklin College in Athens, to engage a gardener for the college botanical garden. A young Englishman, John Bishop, accordingly was hired in New York, booked passage along with the Princes on the ill-fated *Home*, and was one of the few survivors.

In 1883, retired and living in Atlanta, John Bishop told the story of the tragic disaster to three Prince grandchildren who visited him there. It was he who had identified the bodies of the Princes, which had washed ashore. They were buried in North Carolina, but later Oliver Jr. had their bodies brought back to Macon and buried in a family plot in Rose Hill Cemetery. A monument was erected there by the three children in memory of their parents, with the inscription: "They were lovely and pleasant in their lives and in their death they were not divided," a paraphrase of a verse in the Book of Samuel.

Today, there is very little remembrance of Oliver Hill-house Prince, although he was a man of many talents. No male descendant with the surname remains, and only a street in Athens and a small park in Macon bear his name. Of the many all but forgotten words written about Oliver Prince, perhaps the most memorable was the simple statement of a contemporary who noted that coupled with a superb sense of humor he had a "great kindness of heart."

NOTES TO PART II

1. The family had other letters from Edgar Allan Poe, but in 1877 they were lent to William F. Gill to include in a book, *Gill's Life of Poe*, which he was writing. After the book was published, the letters were never returned, Gill maintaining they were destroyed in a fire which occurred in his home. In recompense, he sent the family an inscribed copy of the book.

2. A will was drawn by Prince and is among his existing papers. It was canceled by him, however, on August 27, 1835, for reasons unknown.

3. The state of Georgia paid $12,450 to cover the cost of printing the second edition of Oliver Prince's digest. The completed volumes began arriving in Macon from Boston in January 1838, according to Washington Poe's records. He became the agent for their sale, and careful entries indicate orders were received from throughout the state during the following years.

4. On May 31, 1861, two days after the date of Fanny's letter, Thomas Edward King was elected captain of the Roswell Guards (Company H, 7th Regiment, Georgia Volunteer Infantry). At the battle of First Manassas (July 21, 1861) he was severely wounded in the leg, and was unable to resume command of his company. He returned to Roswell, to walk on crutches for more than a year. In 1863, when Georgia was threatened with invasion by the Federal Army, he again volunteered his services on the staff of Gen-

eral Preston Smith, and fell with his general at Chickamauga on September 19, 1863. His body was brought home to Roswell, along with his sword, engraved with the inscription, "Use me not without cause, handle me not without honor."

5. On the same day, July 7, Sherman sent the following dispatch to General Halleck: "General Garrard reports to me that he is in possession of Roswell, where were several very valuable cotton and woolen factories in full operation, also paper mills, all of which, by my order, he destroyed by fire. They had been for years engaged exclusively at work for the Confederate government; and the owner of the woolen factory displayed the French flag, but, as he failed to show the United States flag also, General Garrard burned it also. The main cotton factory was valued at a million of United States dollars. The cloth on hand is reserved for the use of the United States hospitals; and I have ordered General Garrard to arrest for treason all owners and employees, foreign and native, and send them to Marietta, whence I will send them North. Being exempt from conscription, they are as much governed by the rules of war as if in the ranks. The women can find employment in Indiana. This whole region was devoted to manufactories, and I will destroy every one of them."

Appendix

Collecting Southern Amateur Fiction of the Nineteenth Century

In an address delivered before the Bibliographical Society of the University of Virginia on November 7, 1951, Howard S. Mott noted:

Nineteenth century amateurs were often a special breed, raconteurs who wrote about small homely matters close to their own backyards. Men with their eyes on a limited audience who would recognize and appreciate the realities as well as the extravagances. They were men of culture and wit. They were artists as fully aware of their roles as social historians as Joel Chandler Harris was with Uncle Remus. It is now becoming more and more apparent that these men were pioneers in preserving the actuality but more than this—the attitudes of a frontier America. They often combined the attributes of the realists and the local colorists.

A Georgia amateur contributed to world literature what may be the first American short story classic, in the satirical sketch variously called "The Ghost of Baron Steuben," "The Oglethorpe Muster," and "The Militia Company Drill." First published in 1807 in the Washington, Georgia, *Monitor*, it was quickly copied in newspapers throughout the country and was within a few months reprinted in pamphlet form in distant Salem, Massachusetts. Its periodical republications over the ensuing years are so many that chronicling them would take a monograph, but in book form it appeared not only in John Lambert's *Travels in the United States* (London, 1810 and following) but also in Gifford's *History of the Wars*

Occasioned by the French Revolution (London, 1817), Long-street's *Georgia Scenes* (Augusta, 1835 and following), and Thomas Hardy's *The Trumpet Major* (London, 1880 and following). Carl J. Weber has given these publications of the story their definitive treatment in an article in *The New Colophon* called "The Ghost in the Barber Shop." Seldom has such a popular story as "The Militia Company Drill" had such a little-known author. Not one of the book publications included his name. Only Longstreet knew the author's name, and he didn't tell; he said it was "by a friend." The friend was Oliver Hillhouse Prince, who, although born in Connecticut, was a prominent member of the Georgia bar, United States senator from Georgia, and compiler of a digest of Georgia laws. Since this amusing little sketch of the drill of a rustic militia has never been out of print in one form or another from the time of original publication in 1807 to the present day, it seems safe to call the story a classic. Unfortunately for aspiring collectors, there are only three known copies of the 1807 pamphlet edition, of which two are in libraries and the third is in a private collection.

THE MILITIA COMPANY DRILL

I happened, not long since, to be present at the muster of a captain's company, in a remote part of one of the counties; and as no general description could convey an accurate idea of the achievements of that day, I must be permitted to go a little into detail, as well as my recollection will serve me.

The men had been notified to meet at nine o'clock, "armed and equipped as the law directs;" that is to say, with a gun and cartridge box at least, but as directed by the law of the United States, "with a good firelock, a sufficient bayonet and belt, and powder with a box to contain no less than twenty-four sufficient cartridges of power and ball."

At twelve, about one third, perhaps one half, of the men

had collected, and an inspector's return of the number present, and of their arms, would have stood nearly thus: 1 captain, 1 lieutenant; ensign, none; fifers, none; privates, present 24; ditto, absent 40; guns, 14; gunlocks, 12; ramrods, 10; rifle pouches, 3; bayonets, none; belts, none; spare flints, none; cartridges, none; horsewhips, walking canes and umbrellas, 10. A little before one, the captain, whom I shall distinguish by the name of Clodpole, gave directions for forming the line of parade. In obedience to this order, one of the sergeants, whose lungs had long supplied the place of a drum and fife, placed himself in front of the house, and began to bawl with great vehemence, "All Captain Clodpole's company parade here! Come GENTLE-MEN, parade here!" says he—"all you that has n't got guns fall into the lower *eend*." He might have bawled till this time, with as little success as the syrens sung to Ulysses, had he not changed his post to a neighboring shade. There he was immediately joined by all who were then at leisure; the others were at that time engaged as parties or spectators at a game of fives, and could not just then attend. However, in less than half an hour the game was finished, and the captain enabled to form his company, and proceed in the duties of the day.

"*Look to the right and dress!*"

They were soon, by the help of the non-commissioned officers, placed in a straight line; but, as every man was anxious to see how the rest stood, those on the wings pressed forward for that purpose, till the whole line assumed nearly the form of a crescent.

"Why, look at 'em," says the captain; "why, gentlemen, you are all a crooking in at both *eends*, so that you will get on to me bye and bye! Come, gentlemen, *dress, dress!*"

This was accordingly done; but, impelled by the same motives as before, they soon resumed their former figure, and so they were permitted to remain.

"Now, gentlemen," says the captain, "I am going to carry

you through the *revolutions* of the manual exercise, and I want you, gentlemen, if you please, to pay particular attention to the word of command, just exactly as I give it out to you. I hope you will have a little patience, gentlemen, if you please, and if I should be agoing wrong, I will be much obliged to any of you, gentlemen, to put me right again, for I mean all for the best, and I hope you will excuse me if you please. And one thing, gentlemen, I caution you against, in particular—and that is this—not to make any *mistakes* if you can possibly help it; and the best way to do this, will be to do all the motions right at first; and that will help us to get along so much the faster; and I will try to have it over as soon as possible.—Come boys, come to a shoulder.

"*Poise, foolk!**

"*Cock, foolk!* Very handsomely done.

"*Take aim!*

"*Ram down catridge!* No! No! *Fire!* I recollect now that firing comes next after taking aim, according to Steuben; but, with your permission, gentlemen, I'll *read* the words of command just exactly as they are printed in the book, and then I shall be sure to be right.""Oh yes! read it Captain, read it"! (exclaimed twenty voices at once;) "that will save time."

"*'Tention the whole!* Please to observe, gentlemen, that at the word "fire!" you must fire; that is, if any of your guns are *loaden'd*, you must not shoot in *yearnest*, but only make pretence like; and you, gentlemen fellow soldiers, who's armed with nothing but sticks, riding switches and corn stalks, need n't go through the firings, but stands as you are, and keep yourselves to yourselves.

"*Half cock, foolk!* Very well done.

"*S, h, e, t,* (spelling) *Shet pan!* That too would have been handsomely done, if you had'nt handled cartridge instead

---

*A contraction and corruption of "Firelock." Thus: "Firelock," "f'lock," "foolk."

of shetting pan; but I suppose you was n't noticing.—Now 'tention one and all, gentlemen, and do that motion again.

"*Shet pan!* Very good, very well indeed; you did that motion equal to any old soldier—you improve astonishingly.

"*Handle cartridge!* Pretty well, considering you done it wrong end foremost, as if you took the cartridge out of your mouth, and bit off the twist with the cartridge box.

"*Draw rammer!* Those who have no rammers to their guns need not draw, but only make the motion; it will do just as well, and save a great deal of time.

"*Return rammer!* Very well again—But that would have been done, I think, with greater expertness, if you had performed the motion with a little more dexterity.

"*S, h, o, u, l*—Shoulder foolk! Very handsomely done indeed! Put your guns on the other shoulder, gentlemen.

"*Order foolk!* Not quite so well, gentlemen—not quite altogether; but perhaps I did not speak loud enough for you to hear me all at once. Try once more, if you please. I hope you will be patient, gentlemen; we will soon be through.

"*Order foolk!* Handsomely done, gentlemen!—Very handsome done! and altogether too, except that one half of you were a *leetle* too soon, and the other half a *leetle* too late.

"In laying down your guns, gentlemen, take care to lay the locks up and the other side down.

"*'Tention the whole! Ground foolk!* Very well.

"*Charge bayonet!*" (*Some of the men*)—"That can't be, Captain—pray look again; for how can we charge bayonet without our guns?"

(*Captain.*) "I don't know as to that, but I know I'm right, for here 'tis printed in the book; c, h, a, r—yes, *charge bayonet*, that's right, that's the word, if I know how to read. Come, gentlemen, do pray charge bayonet! Charge, I say!—Why don't you charge? Do you think it ain't so? Do you think I have lived to this time o'day, and don't know what charge bayonet is? Here, come here, you may see for yourselves; it's plain as the nose on your fa—Stop—stay—no—

halt! no! Faith I'm wrong! I turned over two leaves at once. I beg your pardon, we will not stay out long; and we'll have something to drink as soon as we have done. Come, boys, get up off the stumps and logs and take up your guns, we'll soon be done: excuse me if you please.

"*Fix Bayonet!*

"*Advance arms!* Very well done; turn the stocks of your guns in front, gentlemen, and that will bring the barrels behind; hold them straight up and down if you please; let go with your left, and take hold with your right hand below the guard. Steuben says the gun should be held, p, e, r, *pertic'lar*—yes, you must always mind and hold your guns very pertic'lar. Now boys, 'tention the whole!

"*Present arms!* Very handsomely done! only hold your gun over t'other knee—t'other hand up—turn your hands round a little and raise them up higher—draw t'other foot back—now you are nearly right—very well done.

"Gentlemen, we come now to the *revolutions*. Men, you have all got into a sort of snarl, as I may say; how did you get all into such a higglety pigglety?"

The fact was, the shade had moved considerably to the eastward, and had exposed the right wing of these hardy veterans to a galling fire of the sun. Being poorly provided with umbrellas at this end of the line, they found it convenient to follow the shade, and in huddling to the left for this purpose, they changed the figure of their line from that of a crescent to one which more nearly resembled a pair of pothooks.

"Come, gentlemen," (says the captain,) "spread yourselves out again in a straight line; and let us get into the wheelings and other matters as soon as possible."

But this was strenuously opposed by the soldiers.—They objected going into the *revolutions* at all, inasmuch as the weather was extremely hot, and they had already been kept in the field upwards of three quarters of an hour They reminded the captain of his repeated promise to be as short as he possibly could, and it was clear he could dispense with all this same wheeling and flourishing, if he chose. They were already very thirsty, and if he would not dismiss them, they declared they would go off without dismission, and get something to drink, and he might fine them if that would do him any good; they were able to pay their fine, but would not go without drink to please any body; and they swore they would never vote for another captain who wished to be so unreasonably strict.

they swore they would never vote for another captain who wished to be so unreasonably strict.

The captain behaved with great spirit upon the occasion, and a smart colloquy ensued; when at length becoming exasperated to the last degree, he roundly asserted that no soldier ought ever to *think hard* of the orders of his officer; and, finally, he went so far as to say that he did not think any gentleman on that ground had any just cause to be offended with him. The dispute was finally settled by the captain sending for some grog for their present accommodation, and agreeing to omit reading the military law, and the performance of all the manoeuvres, except two or three such easy and simple ones as could be performed within the compass of the shade. After they had drank their grog, and had "spread themselves," they were divided into platoons.

" *'Tention the whole!—To the right wheel!*" Each man faced to the right about.

"Why, gentlemen, I did not mean for every man to stand still and turn himself *na'*trally right round; but when I told you to wheel to the right, I intended you to wheel round to the right as it were. Please to try again, gentlemen; every right hand man must stand fast, and only the others turn round."

In the previous part of the exercise, it had, for the purpose of sizing, been necessary to denominate every second person a "right hand man." A very natural consequence was, that on the present occasion those right hand men maintained their position, all the intermediate ones facing about as before.

"Why, look at 'em now!" exclaimed the captain, in extreme vexation—"I'll be d——d if you understand a word I say. Excuse me, gentlemen, it *rayly* seems as if you could not come at it exactly. In wheeling to the right, the right hand *eend* of the platoon stands fast, and the other *eend* comes round like a swingletree. Those on the outside must march faster then those on the inside. You certainly must understand me now, gentlemen; and please to try it once more."

In this they were a little more successful.

"*'Tention the whole! To the left—left, no—right—that is, the left—I mean the right—left wheel, march!*"

In this, he was strictly obeyed; some wheeling to the right, some to the left, and some to the right-left, or both ways.

"Stop! halt! let us try it again! I could not just then tell my right hand from left! You must excuse me, if you please —experience makes perfect, as the saying is. Long as I have served, I find something new to learn every day; but all's one for that. Now, gentlemen, do that motion once more."

By the help of a non-commissioned officer in front of each platoon, they wheeled this time with considerable regularity.

"Now, boys, you must try to wheel by divisions; and there is one thing in particular which I have to request of you, gentlemen, and that is, not to make any blunder in your wheeling. You must mind and keep at a wheeling distance, and not talk in the ranks, nor get out of fix again; for I want you to do this motion well, and not to make any blunder now.

" *'Tention the whole! By division, to the right wheel, march!*"

In doing this, it seemed as if Bedlam had broke loose; every man took the command. "Not so fast on the right!— Slow now!—Haul down those umbrellas!—Faster on the left!—Keep back a little there!—Don't *scrouge* so!—Hold up your gun Sam!—Go faster there!—faster! Who trod on my ——! d—n your huffs!—Keep back! Stop us, Captain—do stop us! Go faster there! I've lost my shoe! Get up again, Ned! Halt! halt! halt!—Stop, gentlemen! stop! stop!"

By this time they had got into utter and inextricable confusion and so I left them.

Bibliography

Library Collections

Etheridge, Douglas Wayne. "Beaumont." Unpublished term paper, August 1974. Mary Vinson Memorial Library, Milledgeville.

Georgia Journal, 1832–35. Milledgeville newspaper on microfilm. Genealogical and Historical Room, Washington Memorial Library, Macon.

Georgia Messenger and *Macon Telegraph*, 1827–81. Macon newspapers on microfilm. Genealogical and Historical Room, Washington Memorial Library, Macon.

Prince, Oliver Hillhouse. Papers. Special Collections Division, University of Georgia Library, Athens.

Government Records

Prince, Oliver Hillhouse, estate records. Bibb County Courthouse, Macon.

Prince, Oliver Hillhouse, and Samuel Rockwell, tax and property records. Baldwin County Courthouse, Milledgeville.

Newspapers and Magazines

Hicky, Louise McHenry. "The Kings of Barrington Hall." *Georgia Magazine*, December 1965.

————. "When the French Flag Flew Over a Georgia Town." *Georgia Magazine*, December 1968–January 1969.

Moon, Fred Denton. "First Business Woman a Georgian?" (Sarah Porter Hillhouse). *Atlanta Constitution Magazine*, 1931.

Shannon, Margaret. "A Georgia Room 900 Miles from Home." (Rockwell). *Atlanta Journal and Constitution Magazine*. June 24, 1973.

Books

Allen, Hervey. *Israfel: The Life and Times of Edgar Allan Poe.* New York: Farrar and Rinehart, 1934.

Boggs, Marion Alexander, ed. *The Alexander Letters, 1787–1900.* Athens: University of Georgia Press, 1980.

Bonner, James C. *Milledgeville: Georgia's Antebellum Capital.* Athens: University of Georgia Press, 1978.

Butler, John C. *Historical Record of Macon and Central Georgia.* Macon: J. W. Burke Co., 1958.

Coleman, Kenneth, and Charles Stephen Gurr, eds. *Dictionary of Georgia Biography.* 2 vols. Athens: University of Georgia Press, 1983.

Cook, Anna Maria Green. *The History of Baldwin County, Georgia.* Anderson, S.C., 1924.

Coulter, E. Merton. *Georgia: A Short History.* Chapel Hill: University of North Carolina Press, 1947.

Gill, William F. *The Life of Edgar Allan Poe.* New York: W. J. Widdleton, 1878.

Gilmer, George. *First Settlers of Upper Georgia.* Reprint. Baltimore: Genealogical Publishing Co., 1970.

Green, Henry D. "The People and the Culture of Early Piedmont Georgia." In *Furniture of the Georgia Piedmont.* Atlanta: High Museum of Art, 1976.

Grice, Warren. *The Georgia Bench and Bar.* Vol. 1. Macon: J. W. Burke Co., 1931.

Hillhouse, James. *Dramas, Discourses and Other Pieces.* 2 vols. Boston: Charles C. Little and James Brown, 1839.

Johnson, Allen, and Dumas Malone, eds. *Dictionary of American Biography.* 20 vols. New York: Charles Scribner's Sons, 1928–36.

Joiner, Oscar H., gen. ed. *A History of Public Education in Georgia—1734–1979.* Columbia, S.C.: R. L. Bryan, 1979.

King, James R. *Memoir of Mrs. Frances Prince King.* Atlanta: James P. Harrison and Co., 1881.

Linley, John. *The Georgia Catalog, Historic American Buildings Survey: A Guide to the Architecture of the State.* Athens: University of Georgia Press, 1982.

———. *Architecture of Middle Georgia: The Oconee Area.* Athens: University of Georgia Press, 1972.

Longstreet, Augustus Baldwin. *Georgia Scenes.* Reprint. Savannah: Beehive Press, 1975.

McCall, Mrs. Howard H., comp. *Roster of Revolutionary Soldiers in Georgia.* Vol. 3. Reprint. Baltimore: Genealogical Publishing Co., 1969.

McKay, John J., Jr., ed. *A Guide to Macon's Architectural and Historical Heritage.* Macon: Middle Georgia Historical Society, 1972.

Mott, Howard S. *Collecting Southern Amateur Fiction of the Nine-*

teenth Century. Charlottesville: Bibliographical Society of the University of Virginia, 1972.

Myers, Robert Manson, ed. *The Children of Pride: A True Story of Georgia and the Civil War*. New Haven: Yale University Press, 1972.

Northen, William J., ed. *Men of Mark in Georgia*. Reprint. Spartanburg, S.C.: Reprint Co., 1974.

Origin and History of the Georgia Academy for the Blind with Documents from the Beginning, 1851 to 1887. Macon: J. W. Burke Co., 1887.

Phillips, Ulrich Bonnell. *The American Historical Association*. Vol. 2. Washington, D.C.: Government Printing Office, 1902.

Prince, Oliver Hillhouse. *A Digest of the Laws of the State of Georgia*. 2nd ed. Athens: Published by the author, 1837.

U.S. War Department. *The War of the Rebellion: A Compilation of the Official Records of the Union and Confederate Armies*. Ser. 1, Vol. 38, Part 5. Washington, D.C.: Government Printing Office, 1891.

Wade, John Donald. *Augustus Baldwin Longstreet*. New York: Macmillan Co., 1924.

Walworth, Reuben H. *Hyde Genealogy*. 2 vols. Albany, N.Y., 1864.

Williams, Edwin. *The Presidents of the United States, Their Memoirs and Administrations*. New York: Edward Waller, 1849.

Wylie, Lollie Bell, ed. *Memoirs of Judge Richard H. Clark*. Atlanta: Franklin Printing and Publishing Co., 1898.

Young, Ida, Julius Gholson, and Clara Nell Hargrove. *History of Macon, Georgia*. Macon: Macon Woman's Club, 1950.

Index

ABOUT THE ENDSHEETS

The map reproduced on the endsheets is the earliest published plan of Macon, Georgia. Published by George Dane, it was printed in color by Simri Rose and Marmaduke Slade in 1826 and shows the town laid out by the first commissioners.

In the upper left-hand corner the map includes the following explanatory notes:

The lots were intended to contain, and do contain about half of an acre each. But the commissioners being aware of the uncertainty of the compass, declared in their report, that the size of the lots should depend alone on the posts, one of which is placed at each corner of every square. The square as shown in the plan, is to be divided in the middle by an alley of 20 feet and another of 10 feet, crossing it at right angles; each of the portions of the square is then to be divided into two equal parts, each of which is a lot, let the size vary as it may from half an acre.

If a post should happen to be missing, its place is to be ascertained from the nearest posts that are standing.

The streets as laid down in this plan are wide and narrow alternately—the wide are 180 feet—the narrow, 120.

The commons are 1300 feet in width and situate on the north and west of town.

The lots which are improved are colored yellow—the unimproved—green.

The large figures represent the no. of the square, and the small ones the no. of lots in each square. In some instances the publisher was obliged to omit the no's. and dividing lines between lots, to make room for the names of the owners—But the no's. can be easily ascertained from the general plan of numbering. Where adjoining lots are owned by the same person the dividing line is omitted.

The map is a reproduction of the photostatic copy given by Mrs. Frank F. Jones to the Genealogical and Historical Room of the Washington Memorial Library in Macon and is used here through its courtesy.

On the back of the framed map is attached a further explanation:

The streets are laid off as of today, and with the same names, only Wharf Street is now known as Riverside Drive, and Fourth Street is now Broadway. The squares are numbered as of today, and each square divided into eight lots. At the foot of Fourth Street was "Lamar" wharf, and "Rowland Wharf" was just below Fifth Street bridge.

Among the many lot owners are the familiar names of Robert Coleman, John T. Lamar, Thomas Napier, Matthew Robertson, Marmaduke Slade, David Ralston, and Charles J. McDonald. A close study of the lots reveal many family pioneers who built Macon.

A PLAN OF TH

BIBB C

LAID OFF ACCORDING
OF D

PUBLISHED BY GEORGE DANE.
ROSE & SLADE, PRINTERS, MACON. 182

WEST COMMON.

PINE

STREET

1 2 3 4	1 2 3 4	1 2 3 4	1 2 3 4	1 2
31	52	33	34	55
6 7 8 5	6 7 8 5	6 7 8 5	8 7 8 5	8 7

PLUMB

1 2 3 4	1 2 3 4	1 2 3 4	1 2 3 4	1 2
50	49	48	47	46
6 7 8 5	6 7 8 5	6 7 8 5	8 7 8 5	8 7

POPLAR

1 2 3 4	1 2 3 4	1 2 3 4	1 2 3 4	
31	32	33	34	CHUR SQUA
8 7 8 5	8 7 8 5	8 7 8 5	8 7 8 5	

CHERRY

1 2 3 4	1 2 3 4	1 2 3 4	1 2 3 4	1 2
30	29	28	27	26
8 7 8 5	8 7 8 5	8 7 8 5	8 7 8 5	8 7

MULBERRY

1 2 3 4	1 2 3 4	1 2 3 4	1 2 3 4	1 2
11	12	13	14	15
8 7 8 5	8 7 8 5	8 7 8 5	8 7 8 5	8 7

WALNUT

1 2 3 4	1 2 3 4	1 2 3 4	1 2 3 4	1 2
10	9	8	7	6
8 7 8 5	8 7 8 5	8 7 8 5	8 7 8 5	8 7

ELEVENTH TENTH NINTH EIGHTH SEVENTH

WHARF

OCMULGEE